Daniel Webster
and a Small College

Daniel Webster
and a Small College

BY JOHN C. STERLING

HANOVER · NEW HAMPSHIRE

Dartmouth Publications

MCMLXV

Contents

The publisher gratefully acknowledges a debt to the Yale University Library and The Boston Public Library for permission to reproduce documents from the Goodrich and Choate papers in their collections. The valuable aid given by Mr. James Tanis, Yale University Librarian, Miss Dorothy W. Bridgwater, Assistant Head of the Reference Department, and the staff of the Historical Manuscripts Division; and by Mr. John Alden, Keeper of Rare Books, Boston Public Library, is particularly appreciated.

PROLOGUE

Daniel Webster—The Early Years

ON a summer afternoon in 1790, a frail, black-eyed boy, barefooted and dressed in a tow shirt and coarse cassimere trousers, stepped out of his father's tavern at Salisbury Lower Village, in the upper valley of the Merrimack River. Across the highway was the general store kept by his schoolteacher, William Hoyt, filled with tempting things to eat and wear. There his glance fell on a novelty,—a large cotton handkerchief, crudely printed on both sides,— and, having already a passion for literature, he bought it with the coins which were jingling in his pocket. What he saw was the text of the Federal Constitution, which had recently been ratified by the states and was being circulated in this quaint fashion. Then and there he sat down under a spreading elm and read it through.*

Webster was then eight and a half years old.

His father Ebenezer Webster was of the fourth generation of Websters that had lived in New England—mostly in New Hampshire. Ebenezer had fought against the Indians with the famous Rogers Rangers. Later, he served under General Jeffrey Amherst in Canada, returning as captain. Still later, he joined the Continental army. For a while he served directly under General Washington around Boston. Without any schooling, he had taught himself to read and to write. He became a leading citizen and a respected judge. His first wife died, leaving Ebenezer with three small children. He soon remarried, this time to a thirty-seven-year-old spinster. Daniel, on January 18, 1782, became the fourth child of that second marriage. By this time Ebenezer had built a frame house in Salisbury Lower Village, where the Pemigewasset and the Winnepesaukee Rivers flow together to make the Merrimack, near Frank-

* *Daniel*, 1930. [Footnote references to sources are abbreviated and refer to the chronological "List of Works Consulted" on page 57. Thus "*Daniel*, 1930" refers to *Daniel Webster* by Claude Moore Fuess, published in Boston by Little, Brown in 1930.]

1

lin about twenty miles north of Concord, New Hampshire. For fifteen years Daniel's home was to be conducted as a tavern.

During Webster's early boyhood the roads in the area were mostly Indian trails. Then came the wider paths, with sections of corduroy road, for the ox-drawn two-wheelers. Finally, the turnpikes came to Boscawen—and with these rough and dangerous roads came the stagecoach. People in the back country lived by the road. The tavern keeper was important and so was the teamster.

The tavern keeper was ". . . a man who deserves special mention in passing, for he was a major medium of communication through whom the news of the day was spread. Coming as he did into contact with leaders in politics, in business and in law, the tavern keeper sharpened his wits and grew wise in counsel. Frequently he was the most influential man in town, prominent in local affairs. His tavern was of great social and economic importance in the community."[1]

The teamster was indispensable to the back country. Whatever the farms produced could be sold in the cities—iced meat and poultry and wild game, firkins of butter, cheese, hides, and crude cloth. "Every day, Sunday included, the teams passed through the towns lying along the turnpikes; and no vocation called for more robust men than that of teamster. Long whip in hand, the drivers strode beside their teams, twenty miles a day on an average. The whip was their badge of office, seldom applied to a horse. The teamsters' calling demanded assets other than brawn; keen traders they must be, to sell advantageously the goods they carried to town, and to choose wisely for the return trip."[2]

Daniel, as the son of a tavern keeper, was to know these sturdy drivers, who invariably carried their own food but paid ten cents a night to stretch out on the floor and sleep. He heard of glamorous faraway places—Exeter, Portsmouth, and Boston. In turn, Daniel would read to the guests and would recite from the Bible.

"The forces to which Daniel was susceptible came from nature, from humanity, and from books, and he profited by them all."[3] He also was to ab-

1. *Hanover*, 1961; article by Armstrong Sperry.   3. *Daniel*, 1930.
2. *Ibid.*

sorb some basic natural philosophies. From nature he was to learn a love of the land—the mountains, the streams, and the woods. "Daniel never forgot how, when the Merrimack was teeming with fish in the spring, the shad, on reaching the junction of the two streams which formed the larger river, went up the Winnepesaukee to the warmer waters of the lake, while the salmon sought the colder Pemigewasset rushing down from the mountains."[4] From the passing travelers at the inn he was to learn about humanity. From books, especially, he was to learn. So few were available, they were not just to be read; they were often to be absorbed.

Webster himself wrote, "I read what I could get to read, went to school when I could, and when not at school, was a farmer's youngest boy, not good for much for want of health and strength, but expected to do something."[5]

At the age of fourteen he entered Exeter and studied there for a total of nine months. He left before completing his college preparation. It has been generally agreed that the Webster family's usual financial condition caused that discontinuance of his studies.

Daniel's fifteenth birthday found him teaching school at home in Salisbury. Fortunately, an angel appeared—the Rev. Samuel Wood of nearby Boscawen. The good preacher, recognizing the young man's aptitude, offered to instruct him for entrance to Dartmouth—then the only college in New Hampshire. With his quickness at learning, plus some outside help in Greek, Daniel was ready to apply for admission in the fall of 1797.

At that time, by action of the trustees, it was stipulated that "No person shall be admitted to the Freshman class unless he be versed in Virgil, Cicero's Select Orations, the Greek Testament, be able accurately to translate English into Latin, and also understand the fundamentals of arithmetic."[6]

"Daniel Webster, on horseback, carrying with him his feather bed and bedding, together with a few books, some clothes, and provisions for the journey, rode like D'Artagnan, to seek his fortune. He was now only fifteen years and six months old but he had matured rapidly at Exeter and Boscawen, and diffidence was no longer one of his handicaps."[7] At the time that Daniel

4. *Daniel*, 1930.   6. *History*, 1878.
5. *Daniel*, 1883.   7. *Daniel*, 1930.

Webster entered Dartmouth, John Wheelock, the son of founder Eleazar, had already been the able successor of his father for twenty years.

During Daniel's time at Dartmouth the records were still kept in pounds and shillings. The tuition when he was a freshman, in terms of the dollars of that time, was $13.32 a year. Room rent was from $9.00 to $18.00 a year. Board was around $1.20 a week.

The college was situated in a rural farming community and it adjusted its periods of study to the needs of the community. Graduation was usually in August so that the students could go back home and help harvest the crops. The big vacation was January and February and that was almost the key to Dartmouth's financial existence because the students turned to teaching when the farm boys were not busy with farming.

The courses in college were unbelievably rigid. For three years two-thirds of the time was devoted to Latin and Greek. The rules of behavior were equally rigid. Among other severities "the undergraduate was not allowed to keep or play with dice or cards nor to indulge in any other form of gambling."[8] "As might have been expected, the undergraduate body rose to the occasion and gave the 'executive authority' abundant practice in the administration of discipline."[9]

The student body was made up of farm boys with homespun clothes and country manners. There are many evidences of the fact that the more sophisticated youths from Boston looked down on the unpolished manners of the Dartmouth students and early graduates.

Daniel was to stay the full four years and graduate with the class of 1801. He was a good student but no prodigy. As with many youths of genius he was not especially appealed to by the appointed tasks. He was an acknowledged leader and was honored many times for his speaking ability. "But with all his dignity and seriousness of talk and manner, he was a thoroughly genial companion, full of humor and fun and agreeable conversation. He had few intimates, but many friends."[10] "He was tall and thin, with high cheek bones and dark skin, but he was still impressive. The boys about him never forgot the

8. *History*, 1932.   10. *Daniel*, 1883.
9. *Ibid.*

look of his deep-set eyes, or the solemn tones of his voice, his dignity of mien, and his absorption in his subject."[11]

One of his tutors, Professor Roswell Shurtleff, later said, "Mr. Webster, while in college, was remarkable for his steady habits, his intense application to study, and his punctual attendance upon the prescribed exercises. I know not that he was absent from a recitation, or from morning and evening prayers in chapel, or from public worship on the Sabbath; and I doubt if ever a smile was seen upon his face during any religious exercise. He was always in his place and with a decorum suited to it. He had no collision with anyone, nor appeared to enter the concerns of others, but emphatically *minded his own business*."[12] He enjoyed hunting and fishing and was acknowledged to be unusually skilful at each.

In his junior year, the weekly *Dartmouth Gazette* was started and Webster became assistant editor and "under the pen name 'Icarus' was a regular contributor of poems, moral essays, and political articles."[13] He also, the next year, was a regular contributor to a biweekly publication called the *Literary Tablet*.

While Daniel was still a senior, his older brother Ezekiel entered Dartmouth as a freshman and during his four years there made an outstanding scholarship record. Daniel's parents had made great financial sacrifices to see him through college and they were now making further inroads on their meager capital by sending Ezekiel. It was a great tribute to the parents' understanding of what an education could mean, having been denied one themselves. As the years rolled by, the two boys were to show their gratitude by being most solicitous of their parents.

After graduating in 1801 as a Phi Beta Kappa, Daniel took a teaching offer in Fryeburg, just over the New Hampshire border in what is now Maine. This lasted seven months, until he was offered the chance to "read" law in the office of Thomas W. Thompson back in Salisbury Lower Village and took the opportunity.

For almost two years he studied and was often bored. When he tired of reading Coke or Blackstone, he read poetry and fiction and philosophy. He

11. *Daniel*, 1883.
12. *History*, 1815–1909.
13. *Hanover*, 1961; article by Charles E. Widmayer.

often had doubts that his future was to be in law. He regularly went trout fishing with a book in his pocket—just in case. Fortunately, there came a chance to go to Boston. He talked his way into more reading of the law in the office of a distinguished lawyer named Christopher Gore. After nine months of agreeable study, he was admitted to the bar in Suffolk County, Massachusetts, at the age of twenty-three.

But where was he to practice? That was the question. His father was ill. The family money had been used up to send him and his older brother Ezekiel to college. So he returned to New Hampshire to open a law office in Boscawen, six miles from his home at Salisbury Lower Village. He was no farmer—and the little town of 1,500 souls was no horizon to him after seeing Concord and Exeter and Portsmouth and Boston. Most of his legal cases were simple ones, but he began to know the insides of people and he began to meet outstanding lawyers and politicians.

A year later his father died. Soon thereafter his brother Ezekiel returned. At last there was someone who could run the farm and look after his mother and his two unmarried sisters. Thus, after two and a half years in Boscawen, he was able to leave for Portsmouth—then one of the most important cities in the country and, with a population of about 5,000, the largest community in New Hampshire.

For five years after moving to Portsmouth, Daniel Webster was to pursue private practice. In this he traveled the circuit courts as did other trial lawyers. To cover the five counties involved, he was away a lot. Obviously, he could not carry a research library with him but had to depend on memory and ingenuity and the forceful expression of ideas. Webster later said that he had never met such able legal practitioners as he had been associated with in New Hampshire. Particularly he learned to think on his feet and to moderate the flamboyance which had marked his speaking during college days and the years shortly thereafter. He learned to speak so simply to a jury that his words could be understood. He throve on the continuous practice of law with worthy associates and formidable opponents.

Then came a big day in Webster's life. It was the Fourth of July, 1812. That day, plus another one a month later, was to catapult young Webster, in two giant steps, from an obscure local environment to the national scene.

Without ever having held even the most inconspicuous public office, he was suddenly to be thrust into a position of national political leadership.

The War of 1812 was going very badly. The young nation was ill prepared for it. New England with its dependence on industry and shipping was suffering severe economic woes. Some citizens felt that war was the only cure; others did not feel that way. Webster had felt that the war issues could have been settled by negotiation and that they could still be settled that way.

Independence Day was the usual time for parades and flag waving and patriotic oratory. But in Portsmouth, New Hampshire, on that July 4, there was not to be the customary exuberance. The young man from up-country, with full force, deplored both the war and the conduct of the war. He saw no reason to single out England and not proceed with equal determination against Napoleon's France. And yet after his attack on war itself, and after a long denunication of the administration at Washington, he spoke the ringing words of a statesman. He said:

With respect to the war, in which we are now involved, the course which our principles require us to pursue cannot be doubtful. It is now the law of the land, and as such we are bound to regard it. Resistance and insurrection form no parts of our creed. The disciples of Washington are neither tyrants *in* power, nor rebels *out*.

By the exercise of our Constitutional right of suffrage, by the peaceful remedy of election, we shall seek to restore wisdom to our councils, and peace to our country.[14]

Webster's speech was reproduced in pamphlet form—in two editions. Newspapers throughout New England quoted and applauded. One month later, on August 5, 1812, the county Federalist party met—2,000 strong—in a small village at the geographical center of Rockingham County, New Hampshire. Webster had been appointed chairman of a committee to prepare resolutions. He had written out his recommendations in detail. The committee accepted them and Webster delivered the key speech which was to become known as the "Rockingham Memorial." It was addressed to James Madison, Esquire, President of the United States. This time Webster was more pleading than accusing. However, the facts were substantially the same as those presented in Portsmouth a month earlier.

The Rockingham Memorial went beyond New England. Especially in

14. *Writings*, 1903.

seaports the address gained attention in newspapers. The New York *Evening Post* printed the address in full. The Philadelphia *Freeman's Journal*, among others, gave the speech unstinted praise. Opposition newspapers honored the memorial by especially violent attacks.

At that Rockingham County meeting Webster was asked to run for Congress. At first he refused on the grounds that he was too poor to accept. (A congressman's pay was six dollars a day and travel.) Later, however, he was persuaded to run, and he was elected. Thus did the thirty-year-old country boy, through the clarity of his thinking and the magic of his speaking, become a national figure through two outstanding orations.

In May 1813, Webster took his seat in the House of Representatives in Washington. For four years he was to oppose or support John C. Calhoun or Henry Clay. At that time a freshman congressman was not required by convention to observe a period of silence. Clay, in his first year, had been chosen Speaker of the House. Calhoun, in his first year, had been made chairman of the Foreign Relations Committee. For the first year and a half—until the news of the Treaty of Ghent reached Washington—Webster attacked the administration for the War of 1812 and for practically every piece of legislation that had to do with its operation. He fought the embargo until it was finally withdrawn. He opposed a national draft as being unconstitutional. For the same reason he objected to the closing of ports for sea traffic within a state. In one of his early speeches he presented a number of suggestions which, if followed, he said, would make the war a national affair instead of remaining a "party" war.

After the war, Webster was engaged in legislation that had to do with currency and the tariff. With the country temporarily united, the issues tended to be discussed on their merits rather than from a sectional point of view. On the subject of currency and the national bank, Webster was a conservative. He was a "hard money" man after the manner of Alexander Hamilton. Strangely enough, he who was never able to take care of his own finances was a sound and important influence in national finance. "No small part of Webster's constructive work as a legislator was carried on in the unromantic but exceedingly useful guise of an economist."[15]

15. *Daniel*, 1930.

On the matter of the tariff, Webster was caught in a dilemma. Manufacturers in New England sought protective tariff laws, whereas the shippers wanted a minimum of tariff in order to encourage shipping. Webster tended towards the side of tariff for revenue only and not tariff for protection.

By the time Webster came near the end of his second term, there was strong nationalistic sentiment, and thus the Federalist party had lost its issue. He was spending more and more time in legal matters. In August 1816 he moved to Boston, automatically giving up his chance for re-election in New Hampshire.

During his last year in Congress, strange things were happening in the small New Hampshire college. John Wheelock, the able son of founder Eleazar Wheelock, had served as president of Dartmouth for many years. Time, however, had taken its toll—he had held office too long. He fell out with the trustees. He wanted to run things his personal way and not in the manner advocated by the trustees, and he was ousted. In order to get himself reinstated, he appealed to Governor Plumer of New Hampshire. But his protest to the state took an unexpected turn. The Federalists had just been swept from office and the States Rights party was in complete control. The legislature of the state passed three new laws late in 1816. The state took over control of the college, changed the name to Dartmouth University, proposed major changes in the curriculum and installed John Wheelock as president of the new university.

The atmosphere for successful legal action was very bad. Ex-President Thomas Jefferson, in a letter dated July 21, 1816, stated that the reasoning of the New Hampshire Governor was "replete with sound principles" and that the idea of a self-perpetuating board of trustees assumed that "the earth belonged to the dead, and not to the living."

The old trustees brought suit in trover to recover the possessions that the state had seized. In the Superior Court of New Hampshire the old college lost the decision on a three-to-nothing vote. Webster, called in from Boston at the last minute, played a minor role.

In spite of the fact that the outlook for the small college was dim, for it had no physical assets and no money, it did have a board of trustees with a strong will; it had most of the faculty and almost all of the students. In its darkest moment it had a friend in John Wheeler who lived in Orford, twenty miles north of Hanover, in one of the beautiful houses attributed to Bulfinch. He contributed $1000.00 to the cause. But, best of all, the original college had Daniel Webster.

Webster had been legal advisor to John Wheelock, but when the state intruded, he gave up his allegiance to Wheelock and stood on the side of the old trustees. In the New Hampshire court, and later in Washington, he was cruelly accused of stabbing his Alma Mater.

The issue was appealed to the Supreme Court of the United States. Now a nationally-famed constitutional lawyer, Webster, by 1818, had already been appearing before the Supreme Court for almost five years. At the age of thirty-six, he was ready for his big case—Dartmouth College vs. Woodward (The State of New Hampshire).

CHAPTER I

The Peroration

DANIEL WEBSTER, in March of 1818, at the age of thirty-six, stood silent before the Supreme Court of the United States. He had just finished a more than four-hour argument for the plaintiff in the famous Dartmouth College case.

John Wheelock, son of Eleazar Wheelock, the founder, had served the college well for many years, but he fell out with the trustees both on religious and academic questions and was deposed. He appealed to the Governor of New Hampshire for reinstatement. All he wanted was reinstatement to his office as president, but the State of New Hampshire in its overwhelming political defeat of the Federalist party seized on his appeal as a means for taking over the college.

The State of New Hampshire contended that Dartmouth College had been founded to serve the public and therefore should be controlled by the public. To bring about that change, new laws were passed, additional trustees for control were appointed by the State, and the name was changed to Dartmouth University. The trustees of the old college had brought suit for recovery of the seized assets against the State in the New Hampshire courts and had lost. On appeal the case was carried to the United States Supreme Court. The old college contended that the State had no right to take that which was not their own. With a strictly legal and logical plea Webster had maintained that a charter was a contract, that a contract could not be impaired by a state, and that any regulatory action was a matter for the courts and not for the legislature. He maintained that the action of the New Hampshire legislature in seizing control of the small college was in violation of the Constitution of the United States.

(The decision, almost a year later, was to be five for the small college, one against, and one absent. It was to be the most quoted case in the history of the Supreme Court and, under a free enterprise system, it was perhaps to be the most important.)

There was a hush in the courtroom. The bench and the spectators alike were awe-struck by the depth of the arguments and the magic of the delivery.

Webster, after the long moment of silence, faced the stern and learned Chief Justice John Marshall. In a wholly unpremeditated and brief peroration, he abandoned law and logic. In what was to the Supreme Court an unprecedented emotional outburst, he turned the case into a moral and sentimental issue.

Boldly he challenged the Supreme Court. In his magnetic manner he said that if it destroyed that small college, it would be bound to keep on with its work and destroy all colleges and all privately supported foundations and institutions. Then came his dramatic and memorable phrase.

> It is, Sir, as I have said, a small college.
> And yet *there are those who love it!*

Thirty-four years later, after Webster had died, those words were, for the first time, reported and became a matter of record. That thirty-four-year span is a key factor in this narrative.

There were no court stenographers at that time—each justice took his own notes.

Although people in general have accepted this quotation as being authentic, the hiatus between the delivery and the much later recording of the words has been the basis for doubt among some historians of the college and biographers of Daniel Webster.

Among the causes for scholarly questioning of the authenticity of the reported words, is the fact that Webster during his own lifetime failed to mention the peroration or its substance. Between the time of Webster's plea in March of 1818 and the court's decision in February of 1819, there was published a lengthy document edited by one Timothy Farrar, who had been Webster's law partner during the several years spent in Portsmouth, New Hampshire. It was a compilation called *Dartmouth College vs. Woodward.*[1] Web-

---

1. Woodward was treasurer of the new Dartmouth University.

ster participated in the preparation of that record as did the other three lawyers concerned with the argument before the Supreme Court at Washington. Webster in the record of his own appeal made no mention of his peroration. However, in a letter to a lawyer friend he wrote that he had prepared this summary of the case "with all the nonsense left out."

In 1830 there was published *Speeches and Forensic Argument, Daniel Webster*, Volume I. Five years later there was published *Speeches and Forensic Argument, Daniel Webster*, Volume II. In 1851, a year before he died, there was published *The Works of Daniel Webster*, six volumes, with a biographical memoir of Webster by Edward Everett. In none of these volumes was there any mention of the peroration in the Dartmouth College case, and, of course, no mention of the small college phrase.

Interestingly enough, several of the speeches that Webster made while in college had been reproduced in print but none of them were included in any of these volumes produced under his aegis. He himself wrote: "While in college, I delivered two or three occasional addresses which were published. I trust that they are forgotten; they were in very bad taste. I had not then learned that all true power in writing is in the idea and not in the style."

Daniel Webster died at the age of seventy at Marshfield, Massachusetts, in October 1852.

Right after Webster's death, Rufus Choate, noted lawyer, member of the United States House of Representatives, gifted orator, and for two decades a close friend of Webster, delivered a memorial address before the Massachusetts Circuit Court. In that memorial, in speaking of the Dartmouth College case, and in particular of the peroration, he said:

. . . and then [he] broke forth in that strain of sublime and poetic eloquence, of which we know not much more than that, in its progress, Marshall, the intellectual, the self-controlled, the unemotional,—announced, visibly, the presence of unaccustomed enchantment.[2]

Choate, who had been an undergraduate when Webster argued the case, then agreed to deliver another eulogy on Webster at the Dartmouth commencement at Hanover during the following July. Soon after the memorial before the Massachusetts Court, Choate received a long and vivid letter from

2. "Daniel," 1938; quoted from Joseph Neilson's *Memories of Rufus Choate*, Boston, 1884.

Chauncey A. Goodrich, who was then professor of oratory and rhetoric at Yale College. Whether that letter was inspired by Choate's talk before the Massachusetts Court or by the knowledge that he was about to speak at Hanover is not known. That entire speech, including the letter, was reproduced in pamphlet form under the title *A Discourse Delivered Before The Faculty, Students, and Alumni of Dartmouth College Commemorative of Daniel Webster*. In that speech, in introducing the letter, Choate said:

Well, as if of yesterday, I remember how it was written home from Washington that "Mr. Webster closed a legal argument of great power by a peroration which charmed and melted his audience." Often since I have heard vague accounts, not much more satisfactory, of the speech and the scene. I was aware that the report of his argument, as it is [sic] published, did not contain the actual peroration, and I supposed it lost forever. By the great kindness of a learned and excellent person, Dr. Chauncey A. Goodrich, a Professor in Yale College, with whom I have not the honor of a personal acquaintance, although his virtues, accomplishments, and most useful life, were well known to me, I can read to you the words whose power, when those lips spoke them, so many owned, although they could not repeat them.

Here is reproduced, in facsimile, those pages in Choate's pamphlet that became the reference for future historians and biographers.

Choate had altered the original Goodrich letter by additions and deletions and by rearrangements of the sequence of several parts. However, he in no way changed the sense nor did he alter the Webster quotations as reported by Goodrich.

For many years after Choate's memorial, the Goodrich letter, with its Webster quotes, went practically unnoticed by writers. In 1901, almost fifty years after the Choate memorial, there was a two-day celebration at Dartmouth, on the one hundredth anniversary of Webster's graduation. Then, if ever, would Webster lore be covered from all angles. One of the many speakers said that while the college was now large, there were still those that loved it. Another mentioned the Goodrich letter but did not quote from it. No speaker, however, put the words "small college" and "love" together in a single phrase.

There were a number of compilations of Webster's letters that were published after his death, culminating in the so-called National Edition, *The Writings and Speeches of Daniel Webster* (1903) — eighteen volumes. This

ington, Livingston, Johnson, Story, Todd, and Duvall — a tribunal unsurpassed on earth in all that gives illustration to a bench of law, and sustained and venerated by a noble bar. He had called to his aid the ripe and beautiful culture of Hopkinson; and of his opponents was William Wirt, then and ever of the leaders of the bar, who, with faculties and accomplishments fitting him to adorn and guide public life, abounding in deep professional learning, and in the most various and elegant acquisitions — a ripe and splendid orator, made so by genius and the most assiduous culture — consecrated all to the service of the law. It was before that tribunal, and in presence of an audience select and critical, among whom, it is to be borne in mind, were some graduates of the college, who were attending to assist against her, that he opened the cause. I gladly proceed in the words of Mr. Goodrich.

" Before going to Washington, which I did chiefly for the sake of hearing Mr. Webster, I was told that, in arguing the case at Exeter, New Hampshire, he had left the whole court room in tears at the conclusion of his speech. This, I confess, struck me unpleasantly — any attempt at pathos on a purely legal question like this, seemed hardly in good taste. On my way to Washington, I made the acquaintance of Mr. Webster. We were together for several days in Philadelphia, at the house of a common friend; and as the college question was one of deep interest to literary men, we conversed often and largely on the subject. As he dwelt upon the leading points of the case, in terms so calm, simple, and precise, I said to myself more than once, in reference to the story I had heard, 'Whatever may have seemed appropriate in defending the college at *home,* and on her

own ground, there will be no appeal to the feelings of
Judge Marshall and his associates at Washington.' The
Supreme Court of the United States held its session, that
winte . in a mean apartment of moderate size — the
Capitol not having been built after its destruction in
1 14. The audience, when the case came on, was
therefore small, consisting chiefly of legal men, the *élite*
of the profession throughout the country. Mr. Webster
entered upon his argument in the calm tone of easy and
dignified conversation. His matter was so completely
at his command that he scarcely looked at his brief, but
went on for more than four hours with a statement so
luminous, and a chain of reasoning so easy to be understood, and yet approaching so nearly to absolute demonstration, that he seemed to carry with him every man
of his audience without the slightest effort or weariness
on either side. It was hardly *eloquence*, in the strict sense
of the term; it was pure reason. Now and then, for a
sentence or two, his eye flashed and his voice swelled
into a bolder note, as he uttered some emphatic thought;
but he instantly fell back into the tone of earnest conversation, which ran throughout the great body of his
speech. A single circumstance will show you the clearness and absorbing power of his argument.

" I observed that Judge Story, at the opening of the
case, had prepared himself, pen in hand, as if to take
copious minutes. Hour after hour I saw him fixed in
the same attitude, but, so far as I could perceive, with
not a note on his paper. The argument closed, and *I*
could not discover that he had taken a single note. Others
around me remarked the same thing, and it was among
the *on dits* of Washington, that a friend spoke to him of
the fact with surprise, when the Judge remarked, 'every
thing was so clear, and so easy to remember, that not

a note seemed necessary, and, in fact, I thought little or nothing about my notes.'

"The argument ended. Mr. Webster stood for some moments silent before the Court, while every eye was fixed intently upon him. At length, addressing the Chief Justice, Marshall, he proceeded thus:—

"'This, Sir, is my case! It is the case, not merely of that humble institution, it is the case of every college in our land. It is more. It is the case of every eleemosynary institution throughout our country—of all those great charities founded by the piety of our ancestors to alleviate human misery, and scatter blessings along the pathway of life. It is more! It is, in some sense, the case of every man among us who has property of which he may be stripped, for the question is simply this: Shall our State Legislature be allowed to take *that* which is not their own, to turn it from its original use, and apply it to such ends or purposes as they, in their discretion, shall see fit!

"'Sir, you may destroy this little institution; it is weak; it is in your hands! I know it is one of the lesser lights in the literary horizon of our country. You may put it out. But if you do so, you must carry through your work! You must extinguish, one after another, all those great lights of science which, for more than a century, have thrown their radiance over our land!

"'It is, Sir, as I have said, a small college. And yet, *there are those who love it* ——.'

"Here the feelings which he had thus far succeeded in keeping down, broke forth. His lips quivered; his firm cheeks trembled with emotion; his eyes were filled with tears, his voice choked, and he seemed struggling to the utmost simply to gain that mastery over himself which might save him from an unmanly burst of feeling. I will not attempt to give you the few broken words of tenderness in which he went on to speak of his attachment to the college. The whole seemed to be mingled throughout with the recollections of father, mother, brother, and all the trials and privations through which he had made his way into life. Every one saw that it was wholly unpremeditated, a pressure on his heart, which sought relief in words and tears.

"The court room during these two or three minutes presented an extraordinary spectacle. Chief Justice Marshall, with his tall and gaunt figure bent over as if to catch the slightest whisper, the deep furrows of his cheek expanded with emotion, and eyes suffused with tears; Mr. Justice Washington at his side, with his small and emaciated frame and countenance more like marble than I ever saw on any other human being—leaning forward with an eager, troubled look; and the remainder of the Court, at the two extremities, pressing, as it were, toward a single point, while the audience below were wrapping themselves round in closer folds beneath the bench to catch each look, and every movement of the speaker's face. If a painter could give us the scene on canvas—those forms and countenances, and Daniel Webster as he then stood in the midst, it would be one of the most touching pictures in the history of eloquence. One thing it taught me, that the *pathetic* depends not merely on the words uttered, but still more on the estimate we put upon him who utters them. There was not one among the strong-minded men of that assembly who could think it unmanly to weep, when he saw standing before him the man who had made such an argument, melted into the tenderness of a child.

" Mr. Webster had now recovered his composure, and fixing his keen eye on the Chief Justice, said, in that deep tone with which he sometimes thrilled the heart of an audience : —

"'Sir, I know not how others may feel,' (glancing at the opponents of the college before him,) 'but, for my-self, when I see my alma mater surrounded, like Cæsar in the senate house, by those who are reiterating stab upon stab, I would not, for this right hand, have her turn to me, and say, *Et tu quoque mi fili! And thou too, my son !*'

" He sat down. There was a deathlike stillness throughout the room for some moments; every one seemed to be slowly recovering himself, and coming gradually back to his ordinary range of thought and feeling."

It was while Mr. Webster was ascending through the long gradations of the legal profession to its highest rank, that by a parallel series of display on a stage, and in parts totally distinct, by other studies, thoughts, and actions he rose also to be at his death the first of Amer-ican Statesmen. The last of the mighty rivals was dead before, and he stood alone. Give this aspect also of his greatness a passing glance. His public life began in May, 1813, in the House of Representatives in Congress, to which this State had elected him. It ended when he died. If you except the interval between his removal from New Hampshire and his election in Massachusetts, it was a public life of forty years. By what political morality, and by what enlarged patriotism, embracing the whole country, that life was guided, I shall con-sider hereafter. Let me now fix your attention rather on the magnitude and variety and actual value of the

monumental work included speeches which had already been published and many letters that in the meantime had come to light. In none of the letters was there any reference to the peroration. However, there was included a copy of the Goodrich letter as published in the Choate pamphlet.

In 1913, John King Lord wrote a long and able chronicle of the college. Although he devoted 113 pages to the Dartmouth College case, there was no mention of the Goodrich letter.

While the historians were ignoring the Webster quotation and generally neglecting the letter as a whole, the undergraduates were using the quotable words both in banter and in seriousness. Just when did the students begin to use the phrase? It was probably on the day and hour that the small college started to be small by choice instead of by circumstance, and when its remoteness began to be an asset instead of a liability.

At any rate, when the small college expression began to mean something, its authenticity was questioned publicly for the first time.

It wasn't until 1919, a full sixty-five years after Choate had given wings to the Goodrich letter, that E. S. Corwin in *John Marshall and The Constitution* wrote:

Whether this extraordinary scene first described thirty-four years afterwards, by a putative witness of it, ever really occurred or not, it is today impossible to say.

In 1930, there was published a scholarly two-volume biography entitled *Life of Daniel Webster* by Claude Moore Fuess, then the distinguished headmaster of Andover Academy. Dr. Fuess at that time wrote:

Webster's plea on that March afternoon was not all logic. In his Memorial Oration delivered on Webster in 1853, at Hanover, Rufus Choate, that eccentric but silver-tongued genius, quoted a version of Webster's peroration in his Dartmouth College Argument, sent to him by Professor Chauncey A. Goodrich, of Yale, who went to Washington in 1818 as the representative of his institution, the interests of which were likely to be affected.

Between 1818 and 1853, thirty-five years had gone by. Goodrich was a professor of oratory and a brilliant speaker. Choate had a vivid and romantic imagination. It is highly improbable that either could have quoted Webster's exact words. But the famous passage as repeated by Choate in the College Church on Hanover Green, is what Webster might have said, even if he did not employ the precise phrasing which Choate puts into his mouth. The story, moreover, has become so bound up with Websterian tradition that it is almost irreverent to cast doubt on its verbal authenticity.

Two years before, Dr. Fuess had published a biography of Choate titled *Rufus Choate: The Wizard of The Law*. He wrote that Goodrich "preserved for posterity Webster's peroration with its memorable sentence, 'It is, Sir, as I have said, a small college; and yet there are those who love it.' Had it not been for Choate, this utterance might have been lost in the 'dark backward and abysm of time.' " Fuess raised no question of authenticity. Why did he do so two years later in his *Life of Daniel Webster*? Probably, it was because in his Webster he wrote at much greater length with abundant material from which to completely annotate his biography. Choate was not a preserver of records, while Webster was a saver. When it came to documenting the quotes from the Webster peroration, he realized that there was no evidence at all except the Goodrich report made long afterwards. Also, in his biography of Choate he was talking about the single "memorable" phrase. Whereas in his biography of Webster he was probably thinking of two paragraphs of quotation.

In 1932, Leon Burr Richardson, a professor at Dartmouth, published an outstanding two-volume *History of Dartmouth College*. In it he said:

This marvelous description was written the year after Webster's death by one who was himself a master of stately phrase; it depends for its accuracy upon the memory of another concerning an event which had taken place more than thirty years before. How much of it is from Choate, how much from Goodrich, how much from Webster? Even if that question is satisfactorily answered, he of a critical frame of mind may ask what this high emotion has to do with the decision by the Supreme Court of the United States of a question of constitutional interpretation. By this time our mood may be one of exasperation at the questioner. We may, for once, abandon an attitude of skeptical suspicion. Undoubtedly Goodrich conveyed a true picture of the atmosphere of the occasion and of the impression made by the advocate upon those who heard him. That impression is all that is of importance, and with clear conscience we may resolve to allow no questions of literal exactness to interfere with our enjoyment of this marvelously painted picture or to diminish our conception of the essential greatness of its central figure.

The raised eyebrows from such scholars were important. In the future, anyone writing about the Supreme Court, or of Daniel Webster, or of Dartmouth College would automatically place reliance on their worthy opinions.

It seems certain that those who raised the issue of the thirty-four-year span were referring to the entire two paragraphs of quotes as reported by

Goodrich. The first paragraph of these quotes was 220 words, and the second paragraph was forty-nine words. It would be easy to make a case as to the authenticity of both paragraphs in full. However, this study will concern itself only with the single "small college" phrase, because that is the only part that has become widely significant.

No search for a famous phrase would be complete without a look into Bartlett's *Familiar Quotations*. The thirteenth or centennial edition (1955) gives a whopping thirty-four quotes from Daniel Webster, but there is not a word about a "small college" or "love." Certainly Bartlett's did not rule out a quotation because the appeal was to one college only. The favorite quotation of Williams College was included. It was from James A. Garfield in 1871. He was the president of that college. "Give me a log hut, with only a single bench, Mark Hopkins on one end and I on the other, and you may have all the buildings, apparatus and libraries without him." Nor was Dartmouth overlooked, for there appeared the first verse of Richard Hovey's "Eleazar Wheelock Was A Very Pious Man."

There could be two possible ways of removing the doubts. One would be to discover material that had not been available to the doubters. Another way would be to study the available evidence more closely than had been done by others who were regarding the authenticity as an incident and not as the whole objective.

CHAPTER II

The Search

SOON after doubts had been raised as to the authenticity of what was by then Dartmouth's favorite quotation, I played a minor part. My contribution, at that time, was to offer encouragement while someone else did the research.

I had a friend in the late Carroll A. Wilson. He was an honor graduate of Williams College and Harvard Law School. He not only had been a Rhodes Scholar but for years was head of the committee that selected the Rhodes Scholars. He was distinguished in a number of intellectual fields and an authority on American first editions. At one time he was in the process of researching for the origin in print of many famous quotations. The result was an exhibition, *First Appearance in Print of Some Four Hundred Quotations* (Wesleyan University, 1935). I had urged him to expend special effort on Webster's "small college" quotation. He did just that. He made a very important discovery. He found the somewhat mutilated original Goodrich letter in the Boston Public Library. As has already been said, it had been altered, principally in arrangement. Out of Wilson's search came an article in *The Colophon* (New Series, Number 1, Volume III, 1938), "Daniel Webster and Dartmouth."[1]

In the course of Wilson's research he confirmed many of the statements that Goodrich had made in his letter. One and only one doubt arose in his mind. Goodrich had written that Webster closed his peroration with a paragraph containing the expression, "Et tu quoque, mi fili!" On the other hand, there was positive contemporary evidence that Attorney General Wirt, arguing for

1. Mr. Wilson also wrote a booklet, *Mark Hopkins and the Log Hut*—a pleasing Williams College traditional anecdote.

18

the state, had used the same classic quote. Could it be that Goodrich had lapsed and credited the line to Webster instead of to Wirt? Wilson renewed his effort. From one library to another he followed the trail. Finally he came up with an eye-witness letter from Salma Hale, a trustee of the new university, to William Plumer, Jr., son of the Governor of New Hampshire. It was written the day of the proceedings and proved that each had said: "Et tu quoque, mi fili!" Goodrich was not mistaken.

Wilson said:

The marvel is that after complete silence in newspapers, official documents, correspondence, biography and reports of speeches, throughout Webster's long life, the quotation comes to light, thirty-four years after the event, almost through fortuity, from a source that is unimpeachable. Dartmouth College, as, thanks to Webster, it still remains, should erect a tablet to the Reverend Chauncey Allen Goodrich.

To me, at any rate, at the end of this investigation, the scene described and the words used in Goodrich's letter to Choate of November 25, 1852, should be taken as gospel.

When Carroll Wilson's *Colophon* article was reprinted in the *Dartmouth Alumni Magazine* five years later in April 1943, there appeared a note written by Claude M. Fuess. In his Daniel Webster biography of 1930, he had raised doubt as to the exactness of the "small college" expression. Here is the note as it appeared in 1943.

AUTHORITATIVE CONFIRMATION

To the Editor:

I have read with very great interest the article by Mr. Wilson in the *Colophon* and believe that he has made a real contribution to Websteriana. The situation based on all the available facts at the time was discussed by me in my *Daniel Webster*, but Mr. Wilson has uncovered some new material. I believe that his conclusion is substantially sound. In other words, I think that Webster really did utter something like the speech which Mr. Goodrich ascribes to him, even though Mr. Goodrich over the lapse of more than thirty years may have forgotten the exact wording. Finally I believe that every Dartmouth man may take some pride in the fact that Webster's speech as traditionally reported probably was actually delivered in that form.

Claude M. Fuess
Headmaster

Phillips Academy
Andover, Massachusetts

Here we have an authority who still had doubts created by the long spread between the Webster plea and the Goodrich letter.

Carroll Wilson had sent photoprints of the altered Goodrich letter both to the Dartmouth College Library and to me. For about twenty years Wilson's pleasing find was apparently to mean nothing in terms of Websteriana. In the meantime the small college quotation was to gain wider and wider recognition —it was used in serious historical references and it was heard in pleasantries.

The *Encyclopedia Britannica*, always with a lengthy sketch on Daniel Webster, did not use any quotation at all until 1929. Then its biography used one quote—"It is, as I have said, a small college, and yet there are those who love it." Since then the phrase has appeared continuously in successive editions.

I can remember leaving the Yale Bowl after the Green had had a good gambol. An Eli quipped, "Don't count me as one who loves it."

In 1956, John F. Kennedy, then a Senator, designated Daniel Webster as one of eight extraordinary public men. In *Profiles in Courage* he wrote:

How he could express almost any sentiments! Ever since his first speech in Congress—attacking the War of 1812—had riveted the attention of the House of Representatives as no freshman had ever held it before, he was the outstanding orator of his day—indeed, of all time—in Congress, before hushed throngs in Massachusetts and as an advocate before the Supreme Court. Stern Chief Justice Marshall was said to have been visibly moved by Webster's famous defense in the Dartmouth College Case —"It is, Sir, as I have said, a small college—and yet there are those who love it."

In *American Heritage* for December 1957 appeared an article, "Great Man Eloquent," by Gerald W. Johnson. It said: "The court was moved by the logic but Webster's passing remark '—those who love her'—hit the country with an impact that no kind of logical exposition could achieve."

There are many other examples of the use of the quotation—most of them amiable. One widely-read fiction writer in an article in the *New York Herald Tribune* (September 19, 1962), pleading to "keep Congress off camera," explained that in spite of the many disadvantages in having Congress exposed to the klieg lights, there occasionally would be an advantage. He wrote: "Everybody would love to be able to tune in on Daniel Webster as he utters for the first time those words that have since become so tiresome when repeated by later generations of Dartmouth alumni."

In a 1962 television broadcast of a Harvard-Dartmouth football game, a background tribute to the Big Green included this statement: "It is, gentlemen, as I said, a small college, and yet there are those who love it." No script writer who was fully informed would have substituted the word "gentlemen" for the word "sir," no matter how logical it would have seemed to be.

In the fall of 1962, a leading news magazine, in describing the new Hopkins Center at Hanover, gave the quotation in full. A leading sports magazine, in an athletics feature, used part of the phrase—"there are those who love it."

In August 1963, as part of a series on famous Supreme Court cases, *American Heritage* published a ten-page feature article by Richard N. Current. The title was spread across two pages: "It is . . . a small college . . . yet, there are those who love it."

To an ear or an eye that is sensitive to the Webster expression, there are other examples. The only point in mentioning them is that if the quote is memorable to those with only a mild interest in Dartmouth, or no interest at all, it is easy to understand that it could have been very memorable to Professor Goodrich, who was interested both in Daniel Webster and in the Dartmouth College case.

By this time the phrase had become so widely recognizable that no one challenged its authenticity. Nevertheless, I decided to keep on from the point at which Wilson had stopped. He had decided that the first appearance in print of the small college phrase was in Choate's pamphlet which printed his Webster memorial address. In his thorough way he had examined many New England publications. But Wilson, it turned out, had overlooked the then entirely illogical possibility of New York.

The first appearance in print was not in Choate's pamphlet, but in the *New York Times*—then called the *New-York Daily Times*—on July 30, 1853. This find was inspired by a small, obscure book called *Reminiscences of the Eulogy of Rufus Choate on Webster* by Charles Caverno, published in 1914. At the time of the memorial Caverno was an undergraduate and sublibrarian. Possibly the book had not been available to Wilson when he made his survey two decades before I started out with my notebook. Caverno said that a clerk of Rufus Choate had sat up all night with a Mr. Raymond of the *New-York Daily Times,* in order to decipher the illegible writing in the Choate manuscript.

Could this be the great Henry Jarvis Raymond of the *Times*—a founder and the editor, a great editor in an era of Horace Greeley and James Gordon Bennett and other notables? What was he doing in faraway Hanover, and what did he write?

The *Times* was in its third year of existence. It had grown to an eight-page daily, six days a week. At two cents a copy its circulation had reached 25,000 —a substantial showing for a conservative newspaper in a city of 500,000.

Thanks to microfilm, it was possible to glance through all copies of the newspaper published up to that time. Not until the Choate memorial was there evidenced any editorial interest in any New England college. Commencement exercises were reported from Rutgers, Columbia, Hamilton, and Union, but there was no word even from nearby New Haven.

Editor Raymond had been brought up in the lake region of western New York state. A graduate of the University of Vermont with no connection with Dartmouth, he numbered among his many personal friends both Webster and Choate. In fact, he had won substantial recognition for his long obituary of Webster in the fall of the preceding year—sixteen columns written against a press deadline. It was "a feat reported throughout the city's newsrooms, and recalled whenever Raymond's achievements as an editor and writer were listed."[2]

The day before the report on the Choate eulogy appeared, the *Times* printed on July 29, 1853, this dispatch. It was dated July 27 and was apparently sent on the morning of Choate's memorial address.

Dartmouth College—A Note Preliminary
Correspondence of the *New-York Daily Times*

[After reporting the overcrowded conditions and the lack of ordinary comforts, the article said:] It must be that the sons of Dartmouth love their mother or they could not submit to these varied and perplexing embarrassments. Secluded from the world as Hanover is—a place that nobody goes to except on purpose—there is no public house that has at all kept up with the spirit of the age. While every other town in the Union has advanced a hundred years within the past twenty-five, Hanover (with the exception of the College building) remains pretty much as she was before a railroad car had uttered its shrill summons to "all aboard."

2. *Raymond,* 1951.

The dispatch in closing referred to the adequate food and the beautiful scenery. It was signed "Your Constant Reader." Either there was someone else in Hanover interested in communicating with the *Times* or Mr. Raymond was indulging in a little whimsy in having this item appear as a letter to the editor.

On the morning of Saturday, July 30, 1853, the readers of the *New-York Daily Times* were greeted by an extraordinary sight. The entire front page of the newspaper and five of the six columns on page two were devoted to Choate's eulogy on Webster. Here follows a part of Raymond's introduction, after a description of the journey from Boston through Webster's birthplace in the lake region at Franklin and the scene at Hanover.

After an opening prayer by Rev. Mr. Fisher, of Cincinnati, the band played a dirge, and then Mr. Choate rose to speak. His appearance, as you are aware, is singularly striking. Of rather more than medium height,—thin, and apparently of feeble frame,—with large eyes, close, curling black hair, a face flexible in all its features, and expression, and marked by evidences of severe and incessant study, and betraying in every movement, and in every glance, the nervousness and intense, energetic earnestness of his temperament, his opening words and manner are quite sufficient to excite expectation of something quite different from the common-places of eloquent public speaking. And this expectation is never deceived. The whole structure of his mind is eminently original. His voice is rich, sweet and strong; his manner, unstudied, sometimes ungraceful from its abruptness and nervous vigor, is always impressive; his sentences, winding into every nook and corner of the subject, and desperately bent, as it seems, upon hunting out and bringing into light the remotest shades and relations of meaning connected with it—long, involved, parenthetical, and often broken apparently, are yet always correct and wonderfully exhaustive; and his language is classical in its words and phrases, and inevitably exact. He is, undoubtedly, the most thoroughly and profoundly educated man in public life; and his orations, no matter what may be the subject or the occasion of them, are masterpieces of a peculiar and consummate art. He resembles Burke more nearly, in many of the great characteristics of his genius, than any other writer; and if he is inferior to him in that unmatched wealth of intellect which marks Burke as the miracle of his age, he is not unequal to him in that profound and pervasive culture which makes itself [sic] in every word he selects, and in every sentence he utters.

One fault he has which no one closely connected with the Press, or conscious of the agency it must exert upon the tone and scope of public thought, can be expected to forgive;—and that is the supreme indifference he shows to the presentation of his speeches to the public eye. He never speaks when he can possibly avoid it, without the most careful preparation; but the moment he has done, he seems to loose [sic] all thought or care for what he may have said. None of his speeches are accessible in books or in pamphlets, although they would stand, if collected, among the best and most instructive productions of English literature;—nor until the recent energy of the Press, somewhat reckless and *outré* in its modes, it must be confessed, but effective in its results, showed him that without some personal care for the matter himself, he must go to the world in the mangled and distorted shape, which was all the desperate, panting, but inevitable Reporters, could possibly give him, could the public get anything from him even in the form of newspaper reports of his speeches. Fortunate in writing a hand which no human being not gifted with Champollion's[3] skill and with more than his patience of study, can possibly decipher,—and speaking with so great rapidity, and using such infinite and apparently inextricable convolutions of style, that a reporter might as well attempt to follow chain-lightning as to report his words; he seemed absolutely on that height seldom attained, where the press could not reach him. But he has been at last forced to yield; the prospect of having his exquisite sentences and sentiments so mangled and butchered for the public eye, that he himself could not recognize, though he could not repudiate them, was too much even for his resolution; and the Press is now indebted to him for manifold courtesies not less serviceable to himself than to the public at large.

I am consequently able to send you a full report of his Eulogy on Mr. Webster, prepared with a good deal of care, and revised by himself for the Press. It will be read, I do not doubt, with universal interest and admiration.

The *Times* then printed Choate's address including the slightly edited Goodrich letter. On the paper's editorial page, on the same day, appeared a lead editorial praising Choate's address. It closed as follows:

We learn from our correspondent, who sends the Report, which has been carefully revised and corrected by Mr. Choate himself, that he was compelled, for want of time, to omit much that he had prepared, especially in regard to certain portions of Mr. Webster's political life, and the specific character of his intellect. The Eulogy will, however, be speedily published in pamphlet form, at the request of the Alumni before whom it was delivered, and this edition will contain the whole as it was written. The report now given is a perfect copy of the Eulogy as delivered.

It seems reasonable to assume that Choate's clerk sat up with Raymond to interpret the writing and that Choate then reviewed the result.

The commencement exercises were reported by the Boston newspapers and

3. French philologist (1790–1832); he deciphered the Rosetta stone.

nearby newspapers in New Hampshire and Vermont. They covered the social aspects of the occasion but not the substance of Choate's address. However, the *Boston Transcript* did carry excerpts from Choate's Eulogy for ten issues, but there was no trace of any excerpt from the Goodrich letter.

The discovery of the reporting by the *New-York Daily Times* was exciting. It had produced conclusive evidence for when the small college expression first appeared in print, but it did not help in proving the authenticity of the quotation.

CHAPTER III

The Story of the Goodrich Papers

IN a footnote of the Wilson *Colophon* article appeared these words: "The Goodrich family papers were carefully preserved for many years, but were unfortunately destroyed by fire, except for a period having no bearing on this story, in 1919." Inquiries to an associate of Wilson's, who participated in the research, to the executor of his will, and to various fellow scholars, gained no information about the fire.

Wilson's reference to the Goodrich family papers and the fire led me to the Historical Manuscripts Division of the Yale University Library in the hope of finding some clue as to the fire. The Goodrich family papers were there but among them there was nothing that had any bearing on the Dartmouth College case and there was no mention of any fire. The Yale Library, through the co-operation of Howard B. Gotlieb, Archivist of the University, searched various files including the columns of the New Haven newspapers, but still no clue to the fire came to light.

Until 1942 the Goodrich collection was comparatively small and was made up of correspondence involving various members of the family, but with no material from the professor's own working papers. However, among the papers there were twelve letters from Goodrich to his wife. They had been written from Europe in 1825 while he was traveling primarily for his health. The letters were addressed either to "My dear Julia" or to "My dearest Julia." Each was signed in the formal manner of that day, either "C. A. Goodrich" or simply "C. A. G." They were long and detailed. In them Goodrich had underlined single phrases for emphasis just as he later did in his splendid letter to Choate.

In 1942 an important gift to the Yale Library had been made by Goodrich's descendants. It was a substantial collection of Dr. Goodrich's professional papers. They were his notes on lectures and sermons. These professional documents revealed much about Goodrich's mind and character and orderly habits. But they covered only the years 1825 to 1843, thus missing the year 1818— the year of the Dartmouth College case.

The collection was not only a stirring exhibit in itself, but, due to the records of the Yale Library, it provided the names of the donors. The names were to be leads into finding out about the fire.

Correspondence located a great-great-grandson, Chauncey Shafter Goodrich, Jr., in the Institute of Oriental Languages, Cambridge University, England. He knew that there had been a fire, but because he could give no details, he wrote to his mother, Mrs. B. H. Lehman in California. She in turn sent information back to him which he then forwarded to me. Later she sent information direct.

Condensed, the correspondence revealed the fact that Edward Elizur Goodrich, second son of Chauncey Allen Goodrich, sold the family home in New Haven in 1904 and moved to Quito Ranch, Santa Clara County, California. "Everything of value" was packed and shipped to the new home in Quito "including all letters and papers." Some of the collection was stored in the house. "The letters and papers remaining were stored in the barn." The fire took place in the summer of 1919. The ranch house was burned—it and its contents were a "total loss." The barn was spared. The Quito ranch was sold shortly thereafter, and the surviving material was moved to a newer home in nearby Saratoga, California.

It was pointed out to Mrs. Lehman that the lecture notes and sermons in the papers presented to Yale in 1942 covered only the years 1825 to 1843. It was perfectly logical for me to assume that Goodrich, after nine years of professorship, would not suddenly start taking notes and preserving them. Nor was it probable that he would suddenly cease making notes and preserving sermons in 1843 while he still had seventeen active years ahead of him. Regarding this theory, Mrs. Lehman with proper caution wrote, "The missing notes *may* have been in the house itself which would account for their absence." Also she said, "There is no one alive today who knows exactly the nature of the papers that were burned." Mrs. Lehman further stated that no C. A. Goodrich papers have been given to any other institution.

Then there was a windfall. The indefatigable Mrs. Lehman, with renewed interest, searched her home "from cellar to attic," and found an important amount of additional Goodrich family material. This was promptly offered to the Yale University Library, and it was just as promptly accepted. This 1962 addition just about doubled the Goodrich material that had been presented twenty years before.

The newly enlarged collection of Goodrich papers required all of twelve boxes each about the size of two and a half shoeboxes—truly a significant collection. Six of the boxes contained correspondence, mostly having to do with relatives. One box held business papers and one was full of printed material. That left four boxes of sermons and notes on speeches and lectures. The sermons were usually written out in full, almost all by an amanuensis. The notes were phrases or occasional paragraphs in Goodrich's own handwriting.

Most of the notes were in small-sized booklets, carefully stitched together with thread as was characteristic of notebooks of the time. There were outlines on two lectures given at Amherst; one at the Andover Exhibition, 1824; and there was one entitled "Dartmouth Senior, November, 1825"; "Dartmouth Commencement, 1829"; "Dartmouth Commencement, 1830." Many were marked as having been delivered at Yale. Again "Andover, 1831"; "Andover Rhetorical Society, 1832." Some notes said, "Demosthenes." Also there were many general lectures which showed no dates. One was entitled "Observations on Elocution"; another "Lectures on Emphasis"; another "Reason." Also there were "Refutation" and "Conduct of Reply." One particularly interesting collection was "Lectures on American Eloquence I, II, III." Each one of these had about 500 words of notes and occasional full sentences. One note said, "Tariff," "Mr. Webster," "Mr. Clay." Another said, "U. S. Bank," "Mr. Webster," "Mr. Clay," "Mr. Clayton." Another without a title simply had the notes "Mr. Webster," "Mr. Calhoun," "Mr. Clay." Then there were a half dozen lectures on English oratory.

The triumvirate of Clay, Webster, and Calhoun was a natural combination. Webster and Calhoun were born in the same year with Clay preceding them by five years. Clay and Webster died in the same year with Calhoun preceding

American Eloquen—

Lect III

Mr Dexter of Boston

X. End of the war Manufactures and inland
improvements, Mr Clay, Mr Calhoun — Mr Webster
Mr Gaston—

. Missouri Question Mr John Sergeant
Landers. Mr McLean of Delaware—

I. The Greek Revolution Mr Clay. Webster

II. Of the reduction of the tariff. Mr Haynes,
very glowing but eloquent.
Harrison — Mr McDuffie — themselves or carried
by caution — Mr Webster — Mr Clay — Mr Clay too
Delaware

III. The removal of the Cherokees Mr Sergeant,
Elegant, forcible — Mr Storrs—

III. The Removal of the Deposits by
Genl Jackson — Mr Berrien of Georgia.
Mr Clay — Webster & Mr Benny — Goodall
Mr Edward Everett — Elegant, imaginative — clear
    Law of acquisition
    . More recent events —
    . Mr Choate

her York - but Lord Brougham - not I remember
but exceedingly strong -

of Hopkinson on the screw - Son of Judge Hopkinson
on Philadelphia - die with the famous talents
of the Roll of the Rep --

of Mckean or the highest for elegance and face
First known by a pamphlet or Fore you -
Very elaborate. published - it strong - to
with also for Judge Chase - he written defence
= War put early on the Rail -
most Stood difficulty

At the period of the Embargo - 1806 A
arong out of the conflicts between France
and England - Unfortunately have great
facto sympathized with other nation -

In the affairs thing
In 1806 - Embargo - Suddenly put on
to at last rakhued he be for a limited period
A permanent embargo a novelti - off
Offered accordingly by the commercial
of community - Mr J. real Dumas
Very ardent - screw - Mr Giles or the
Abu side - Mr Randolph - opposed the

war - -
His character
considerahoulne a man of shrewy, and crash
mind = gov. by no ordinary law - The
great power was in attack the come
No, and under Mr Adam the admonished
of the Pres. Adam - very powerful - neck
Rep - great power of sarcasm - Keen not
always ready - Here of much beya, man who
meant to insult him - combat her to fight

lmost coincided. But that
ad served in the House of
re and Webster and Cal-
nificent oratorical battles
years for Webster, fifteen
e were the intense golden
at were to mould and test

from notes prepared by
They are from the papers
le in 1962 and were not
he notes on rhetoric and
the same time his many
racteristic we may be cer-
a hurry. His mind would
r "i" and seldom crossed
as usually a quarter of an
s looked like some sort of

r. Goodrich made copious
n. They also showed that
keep reminding him of the

mile here presented, Dr.
outh." There were plenty
ways spelled correctly ex-
paragraph read, "At this
Mr. Clay Calhoun to
var [1812] First known
College Case." Why that
e fact that when I entered
lege as Dartsmouth. This
that in 1905 the Russo-
ned in Portsmouth, New

The second facsimile has a number of interesting points. As was sometimes the case, Dr. Goodrich wrote in short cryptic notes instead of full sentences. He mentions the name of Webster four times, proving that Webster was much in his mind. One interesting sidelight is that in paragraph x, in spelling the word Missouri, he carried on his habit of indicating the first letter "s" with an up and down flourish that said "double." When writing for someone else to read, Goodrich was careful and his penmanship was legible.

Could there be any question that, except for the fire, there would have been another small booklet in the collection? This imaginary little booklet would probably have been about six inches high and four inches wide. There might or might not have been horizontal lines. The booklet perhaps would have been eight to twelve pages thick and neatly sewn together at the lefthand edge with thread going through the holes several times and then tied in a neat knot. What would he have titled it? Perhaps "Washington, 1818." More probably it would have been marked "Mr. Webster, 1818." There would be no running story but many notes. When it came to the word "eleemosynary" he probably would have used, as he had on a number of occasions, the Greek characters for the word from which it had been derived—the old Greek word for "alms." Probably he would have noted the phrase, "Et tu quoque, mi fili." Above all, he would have written, "And yet there are those who love it."— underlined. Altogether perhaps there would have been 400 words of notes.

If this little dream by any chance could have been anywhere near true, and if he had followed his usual custom, the notes would have been saved and would have been available to him when he wrote the letter in 1852, since the fire did not occur until many years later.

The collection as a whole, in addition to being a substantial revelation of Goodrich's scholarship and literary practices, showed conclusively the characteristics of his handwriting as well as the type of nibs or penpoints that he ordinarily used in his pens. Perhaps above everything else the many lectures and sermons proved that Goodrich was no extremist. He was a very believable writer.

Unfortunately, none of the new additions to the collection of lectures had any relation to the years immediately preceding or following the period of the Dartmouth College case. However, there was a big bonanza among the

Goodrich letters. Mrs. Lehman picked it out herself. It was Choate's letter to Goodrich which had not seen the light of day for over 110 years. In it Choate thanked Goodrich for his eye-witness description of the trial scene at Washington and said that, unless Goodrich objected, he would use the entire letter in his forthcoming Webster memorial address at Hanover.

CHAPTER IV

Examining the
One Witness—Dr. Goodrich

IN many a case of adjudicature the verdict has hung on the testimony of a single reliable witness. In the case of the now famed quotation, there is only one witness, the Reverend Chauncey A. Goodrich. It is appropriate that he should be examined both as to integrity and as to competence. He can stand close examination on each point.

Chauncey Allen Goodrich was born October 23, 1790, in New Haven, Connecticut. He came from a distinguished line of scholars. His grandfather was the Reverend Elizur Goodrich, who was married to a direct descendant of Reverend Charles Chauncey, the second president of Harvard College. The grandfather was a preacher, for years, in Durham, Connecticut. For twenty-one years he was a member of the Yale Corporation. At one time he was a leading candidate for the presidency of that institution.

The father was the Hon. Elizur Goodrich who married the daughter of Daniel Allen, a prominent resident of Great Barrington, Massachusetts. This second Elizur was a lawyer. At one time he was Collector of the Port of New Haven. He became mayor of the city. He was a Representative in the United States Congress. For a long time he was Professor of Law at Yale. For thirty years he was Secretary of the Yale Board of Fellows.

Chauncey Allen Goodrich, not yet twenty, graduated from Yale in 1810, as a leading scholar. While in college he adopted a very religious life. His whole energy was to be dedicated to Christian service. In spite of his intense convictions, he developed a tolerance both for the doubters and for the extremists. After graduation he became rector at New Haven's Hopkins Grammar School, which he had attended before entering college.

Two years later he became a tutor at Yale College. While acting in that capacity, he began his studies for the ministry. Fortunately, his guide and mentor was none other than Dr. Timothy Dwight, then president of Yale College. At the suggestion of Dr. Dwight, he began his literary labors by preparing a Greek grammar which was published in 1814. This effort was so successful that it was not only in exclusive use at Yale but was used by other colleges for twenty years.

In 1814 he resigned his tutorship and concentrated on religious studies and on preaching. While attending a winter semester at Andover Theological Seminary, he frequently occupied the pulpit at the Park Street Church in Boston.

The year 1816 was an eventful one. He was ordained into the ministry and accepted a call to preach at the First Congregational Church in Middletown, Connecticut. Also, he married Julia Webster, the second daughter of Dr. Noah Webster,[1] who was to publish the first great American dictionary.

During the following year, he accepted the newly created chair of oratory at Yale—thus becoming C. A. Goodrich, D.D., Professor of Rhetoric.

His routine of duties was something like the following. The Sophomores were instructed by him, through the summer term, in Jameson's Rhetoric. The Senior classes were taught out of a textbook in higher rhetoric and criticism, and read compositions before him which were afterwards criticized in private. The two middle classes, with the Freshmen, were exercised in declamation, with unwearied pains; and with equal labor to himself he introduced that careful preparation for the exhibitions of the Juniors and for the public commencements, which has made the exercises of those public duties so much more of a benefit than they were formerly and so much more creditable to the Institution.[2]

From the beginning the professor taught by example—the examples being the great orations of the past and present. A textbook for seniors was *Demosthenes on the Crown*.

In 1818 the young professor was about to be an observer at a great example; he was to go to Washington to hear Daniel Webster argue before the Supreme Court in Dartmouth College vs. Woodward. He was ready for that event.

1. No kin of Daniel Webster.
2. *Discourse*, 1860.

During the next few years he helped to establish a Theological Department in the college, while continuing his activities as Professor of Rhetoric in the college. In 1821 he was offered the presidency of Williams College, which he declined. Due to ill health, perhaps from overwork, he gave up his work for more than a year, during which time he traveled through many countries in Europe.

In 1828 he purchased the nine-year-old monthly magazine *Christian Spectator*. He turned it into a quarterly and was the sole editor of that flourishing magazine until he disposed of it eight years later. It gained great prominence in the tense theological discussions of the day. In 1839 he had received a new assignment as Professor of Pastoral Theology, a new department that was to become the Yale Divinity School. During the twenty years while he held this professorship, his connection with the college proper did not wholly cease. Every week his voice was heard in the college chapel. His lectures on eloquence were delivered at once to the theological students and to the senior class in college.[3]

Thus it was that Goodrich was to teach oratory for forty years, the duration of his term as Professor of Rhetoric in the college and the period of his professorship in the Divinity School. For one who taught by example, or—as the legal profession would label it—by case history, there must have been many occasions that prompted him to recall the Dartmouth College case, especially since Webster was very prominent during most of Goodrich's teaching career.

In addition to his teaching duties, Dr. Goodrich was called upon continuously for public speaking. He was active in religious societies. For a time the Tract Society of New York engaged much of his attention. Later, after a disagreement on policy, he transferred his allegiance to the Tract Society of Boston. He was a working committeeman in the Bible Society. As if that were not enough, he took active local leadership in the cause of temperance. He still found time to be influential in missionary work.

Goodrich was dedicated to religion. He can be described only as ardent. However, he was tolerant of the various beliefs of the time, and as for individuals, he had a record of "not breaking the bruised reed nor quenching the smoking flax."

3. *Discourse*, 1860.

At the same time that he was absorbed in religious matters, Goodrich did not hesitate to take on the additional burden of various secular enterprises. In 1831, Goodrich composed a series of Latin and Greek lessons. They were written for the education of one of his sons, but they were soon in extensive use.

There were two projects that were to be a strain on his energy as well as an exaction on his working hours. One was the preparation of a major work— *Select British Eloquence*. The other was his years of work on the various revisions of Dr. Noah Webster's *American Dictionary*.

In 1852 he published *Select British Eloquence*. It was in the very year in which he wrote his memorable letter to Rufus Choate. The work was a tome of nearly a thousand pages. It was exactly the kind of opus that would most engage the convictions that Dr. Goodrich held. First there were the principal speeches of Chatham, Burke, Fox, the two Pitts, and Erskine, among others. To these were added biographical sketches and notes. The author's criticisms and summaries were calculated to make the reader understand the backgrounds and the motives of each orator. The whole followed Goodrich's method of teaching by example. The volume met with wide academic approval.

His interest in the dictionaries, once started, was to be lifelong. A dozen years after he had married Julia Webster, came Goodrich's chance to enter the technical world of words. It was in 1828 that Dr. Webster published his first dictionary. It was called *The American Dictionary of the English Language*. It dealt with spelling, pronunciation, and usage. It was published in quarto size in two volumes. It was by far the most ambitious dictionary available. However, at its price of twenty dollars, it was not a widely used lexicon.

Dr. Goodrich "made representations to Dr. Webster that an abridgement would be desirable."[4] Dr. Webster agreed and designated Dr. Goodrich for the task. Soon an octavo edition appeared under the superintendence of Dr. Goodrich, although largely executed by others. "It became his property, and turned out to be a very popular work."[5] His function was especially in orthography and pronunciation. These duties were to prepare him for his later work in lexicography.

In 1840 another unabridged edition was produced by Dr. Noah Webster. Three years later that noted scholar died. Then "it was deemed important

---

4. *Discourse*, 1860.   5. *Discourse*, 1860.

both for the interests of the family and for those of the Messrs. Merriam of Springfield, who had acquired an interest in the work, that a thorough revision of the unabridged dictionary should be attempted, and Dr. Goodrich was requested to undertake the labor. This revision, although he was assisted by several collaborators and scribes, cost unwearied pains and occupied a good part of the working hours of several years. It appeared in 1847, in one volume, small quarto; and being put, by the sagacity of the publishers, into such a shape, and at such a cost that it could be purchased by a large part of the community, it had immense success."[6] At the same time that the large dictionary in a single quarto volume was produced, Goodrich also made thorough revision of the octavo size. Stereotype plates were prepared for use in England and both issues were widely distributed not only in England but in the Dominions. Several years later Dr. Goodrich produced a collection of synonyms that was considered better than other similar compilations in the English language.

The upstanding and learned professor was no ordinary man. But, how about memory—the ability of anyone to remember exact words for thirty-four years? In his letter to Choate, many major points which were in the narrative are amply confirmed by one or more of those who were at the Washington trial. These points are not in dispute. Even the quote from Mr. Justice Story about pen in hand but no notes is confirmed by the Justice's own statement. The reporting in the narrative required only memory of incident or scene, but needed no exactitude of words. Surely no one would question Goodrich's authenticity in the narrative. In his letter to Choate, the professor, in referring to the scene at Washington, wrote, "they [the circumstances] will always live in my memory."

That brings us down to the two paragraphs of quotations from Webster. The first quotation, 220 words in length, began with, "This, Sir, is my case" and included the small college phrase. The second quotation, forty-nine words in length, began with, "Sir, I know not how others may feel." The two combined would not be a memory feat for men who were, in those days, accustomed to memorizing. The two together were just three words less than the somewhat later Gettysburg Address. As has already been stated, it is not the

6. *Discourse*, 1860.

purpose of this discussion to prove that all the words quoted were remembered exactly, even though there is ample logic to support such a contention. For example, how could anyone, especially a professor of oratory, forget Webster's sentimental words about the small college? "It is small"—"one of the lesser lights"—"in your hands"—"you may destroy it." Then, as lightning out of the blue, came the thundering challenge of defiance: "but if you do [destroy it], you must carry on your work! You must extinguish, one after another, all those great lights of science, which for more than a century, have thrown their radiance over the land." Then, abruptly, the one phrase with which we are concerned.

Experts on total recall point out that a phrase tends to become more memorable if it is a highly-charged emotional expression. Also they say that both repetition and association tend to stimulate that memory. Each, in the jargon of the experts, creates "a prepotency for reinstatement to consciousness." Repetition took place in Goodrich's classroom. Each year came a new group. How many times he told the whole story we do not know. But in the files of his own lecture notes, the name "Webster" frequently appears as a reminder.

Association came from the news of the day, and Webster was news. Soon after the Supreme Court case, Daniel Webster was to become the new country's first great "occasional" speaker. "Occasional," as it was called, did not mean infrequent; it meant nonpolitical or commemorative of an occasion. Two years after Webster had moved the court and the audience in the Dartmouth College case, he was chosen to be the orator for the two-hundredth anniversary of the landing of the Pilgrim fathers. That Plymouth address brought fame to Webster as a memorialist in addition to his existing reputation as a forensic orator.

Five years after the case at Washington, Daniel became United States Representative from Massachusetts. This lasted four years.

He was chosen to be the speaker at the laying of the cornerstone of Bunker Hill Monument.[7] Shortly thereafter, he was selected to give an occasional eulogy on the careers of the two ex-Presidents John Adams and Thomas Jefferson, who, by coincidence, had died, hours apart, on the same day, July 4, 1826.

7. Printed copies of his speech carried a cover price of 12½ cents.

For fourteen years Webster was a member of the Senate. Then for two years he served as U. S. Secretary of State, after which he returned to the Senate for another five years. During the last two years of his life he again acted as Secretary of State.

During all this time Webster was to be a leader in many controversies and was to earn recognition as "The Defender of the Constitution." With the preservation of the Union uppermost in his mind, he was constantly compromising on the tariff, on the banking system, on nullification, on abolition, and again on the tariff. "The attention of the nation was focused on the Senate, and focused especially on the three most gifted parliamentary leaders in American history—Clay, Calhoun and Webster!"[8] Webster was continuously in the news.

Both Goodrich's life work as a teacher of oratory and the impact of Webster's activities would surely reinforce his memory.

Insofar as Websteriana is concerned, it was an extraordinary bit of good fortune that there was in Washington such a man as Chauncey A. Goodrich to report the dramatic scene and the moving peroration. It was fortunate because the professor was a man of outstanding integrity and competence. The man who succeeded Noah Webster as the greatest lexicographer of his time would have been extremely careful with words.

Who of those alive at the time that Goodrich wrote the letter would have been the ideal person to testify to the validity of the quotations? It would have been none other than Rufus Choate himself. Choate's letter of reply to Goodrich had remained buried for 110 years and was discovered among the resurrected Goodrich papers in the improbable locale of a small town in California. Reproduced here is a facsimile of Choate's letter.

Here is a translation of Choate's letter which is the result of the efforts of a number of people, including the Goodrich descendant Mrs. Lehman of California and John Alden, Keeper of Rare Books at the Boston Public Library.

8. *Profiles*, 1956.

I hope I shall do nothing inconsistent with your wishes if I introduce your entire description of that scene into the discourse I am to pronounce at Dartmouth College. It is certainly among the most striking in the story of his successes, or of those of any eloquence. And such testimony, from such a source would indeed be Eulogy.

I am with great esteem
Your obedient servant
Rufus Choate

Boston 4 Dec. 1852

Chauncy A. Goodrich, D.D.
Professor &c.&c.&c.

My dear Sir

I have been prevented until this moment from acknowledging the receipt of the book & letter which you have had the great kindness to send me; and now I can scarcely convey to you a full expression of the deep interest with which I have read them. The best selective Collectanea of British Eloquence ever made are here enriched with by far the best helps to their study which I have ever seen; and the English bar & Parliament of our day might learn from your labors, with absolute surprise, that in spite of themselves their race *has been* eloquent.

The destination which you originally designed for this particular copy gives it, if it might be, a special value & an affecting interest.

I cannot sufficiently thank you for the matter of your letter. I have often wished to inquire of Mr. Webster himself what were his thoughts in that celebrated peroration—but could never quite venture on it. He has related in my hearing the effect on the great Chief Justice and from all sources I have gathered that it was among his surer felicities, but your own is the only report from an eye witness with which I have ever been favored. Single expressions, probably inaccurately conceived, were current in college & rest on my memory—but yours is indeed a restoration.

I hope I shall do nothing inconsistent with your wishes if I introduce your entire description of that scene into the discourse I am to pronounce at Dartmouth College. It is certainly among the most striking in the story of his successes, or of those of any eloquence; and such testimony from such a source would indeed be eulogy.

I am with great regard
Your obedient servant
Rufus Choate.

CHAPTER V

Examining the Only Evidence

HAVING examined the only witness, we must now examine the one
and only piece of evidence regarding the small college phrase, the
letter of Chauncey A. Goodrich written to Rufus Choate. In that letter, from memory or from notes or from both, Goodrich described the dramatic scene in the courtroom in 1818, and he recreated a part of the fabulous
peroration. Now we shall deal with the physical aspects of the letter: the
handwriting, Goodrich's own editing before the letter was sent to Choate, and
Choate's changes, some made on the face of the letter and some made through
the use of overlays.

The letter itself was only a small part of the manuscript which Choate had
painstakingly prepared. In its final pamphlet form it was titled *A Discourse
Delivered Before the Faculty, Students, and Alumni of Dartmouth College on the
Day Preceding Commencement, July* 27, 1853, *Commemorative of Daniel Web-
ster*. This manuscript was preserved in a leather-bound volume titled *Original
Ms. of Choate's Eulogy on Webster Delivered at Dartmouth*, Given to the Boston
Public Library by Joseph Leonard,[1] 1868.

The manuscript was entirely in Choate's own handwriting, mostly on light
blue paper, 9¾ by 7¾ inches. In several places Choate had pasted in newspaper clippings with a minor amount of editing. The Goodrich letter itself
was bound into the manuscript (see Appendix).

At this point it became obvious that to make a proper study of the letter itself, as evidence, it would be desirable to restore the Goodrich letter to its
original condition rather than work with Choate's altered version. The altera-

1. Then a Boston book dealer.

tions in Goodrich's letter had been effected in such a manner that experienced people felt that the original letter could not be restored. In the first place, it would be necessary, in four places, to remove the sealing wax with which an overlay had been attached to the face of the letter. (Two overlays had been attached by means of tipping the edges with glue. These presented no problem.) And the paper had been pulled apart in several places during the process of binding the letter into the full manuscript. These damaged parts could be pulled together only by patiently working with the fibers in the paper. However, Boston was fortunate in the possession of one of the few technicians who was skilled in the restoration of art works and manuscripts produced on paper. For years he had worked on all sorts of damaged prints and had become particularly noted for the restoration of marine pictures in water colors. His name: Francis W. Dolloff, Technical Assistant, Department of Prints, The Museum of Fine Arts, Boston. The restored letter itself is now encased in Plexiglas so that it will be preserved for many years to come.

The reproduction of the restored Goodrich letter on the following pages is through the courtesy of the Boston Public Library, John Alden, Keeper of Rare Books, and with the blessing of Robert B. Choate, publisher of the *Boston Herald*, who is of the Rufus Choate family.

The heavy lines crossing out paragraphs and lettered "a" and "b" were Choate's markings to transfer those paragraphs to a different sequence. The first two paragraphs which were completely eliminated are not crossed out at all, but the four marks caused by the sealing wax which made the overlay secure are clearly visible on the first page of the letter. The several places in which Choate made slight changes are clearly indicated by his heavy penpoint and his scrawl.

While it has no bearing on the reading of the letter, it is interesting to note on page 1 the skillful workmanship involved in restoring the letter. The irregular lines of the restoration are clearly visible. Also, on page 2, on the right-hand side, there are the clear lines of a further pulling together of the manuscript.

Goodrich's amanuensis had started the letter with "My dear Sir" and ended it with "Very truly yours." The unmistakable handwriting with the stub pen was found in other Goodrich writings among the family papers at the Yale

Library. Perhaps Goodrich first wrote the letter in longhand and then had it copied. For instance, the last word in the fourth line is "for" and the same word starts the fifth line. This seems like a copying error. Or perhaps, if there had been a previous copy, Goodrich may have used the old bookish practice of repeating at the foot the "catchword" that began the new page—just to keep the sequence. But it makes no difference as to whether or not there was a first draft. The point is that after the amanuensis had finished, Goodrich took over.

How much he changed in the editing we cannot be absolutely sure. But we do know that he did edit. On the first page there are three places in which parentheses were added. It looks very much as if they had been executed by Goodrich's fine pen, but we cannot be sure. Also, running all through the letter are various underlinings. They were clearly put in by the fine pen of Goodrich. They were undoubtedly put in because they seemed to indicate the most important words. As Goodrich himself said in his letter describing Webster's delivery, "Now and then, for a sentence or two, his eye flashed and his voice swelled into a bolder note, as he uttered some emphatic thought." Goodrich certainly was not underlining the words to indicate to Choate what to emphasize. They were important because they were more meaningful, or more memorable, or both. There were two strokes of the pen that were especially significant. One was the underlining of the phrase "that which is not their own." This had been a telling argument in Webster's plea before the Supreme Court.

The small college, just across the Connecticut River from Vermont, had been the recipient of a generous land grant from that state, probably because of gratitude for educational facilities available to its own Green Mountain boys. Webster asked if anyone could presume that Vermont would present its own lands to the State of New Hampshire.

The other important underlining was of the words "there are those who love it." That was the highly surcharged statement that did not belong in any legal argument. One might well ask, "And why didn't Goodrich underline the words 'a small college'?" It was because such an underlining would have seemed redundant. The entire peroration was about a small college. Also, the phrase "there are those who love it" would have been meaningless without the words "a small college."

Then there is the matter of quotation marks. Here they may have been

Yale College, Nov 25, 1852

My dear Sir,

I have taken the liberty to send you, through our friend Henry Hill, a book which I have recently published, designed to aid the young men of our country in the study of eloquence. A glance at the preface will show you my plan, and will explain my reasons for for confining the present volume to the orators of Great Britain. The copy sent you is the one originally intended as a tribute of respect and veneration for the greatest of our New England orators. I have felt that it ought to pass into your hands; especially as the City of Boston, and Dartmouth College have called upon you to speak of his greatness and his virtues.

There is a passage in one of the early pages of this work, (the 21st) which reminds me of what I have heard from Mr Webster, when I first listened to his eloquence. It is Lord Belhaven's application of the words, "Et tu quoque, mi ", to Scotland, when "attending the fatal blow and breathing her last", (as he considered it,) under the compulsion which drove her into a legislative union with England. Mr Webster applied them still more beautifully at the close of his argument at Washington in the case of Dartmouth College. In publishing his speech, however, he left out the entire peroration, giving in its place an extract from Cicero, which he probably regarded as a more appropriate conclusion of a strictly legal argument. No hand but his could ever reproduce it; but I am sure you will be interested in a slight sketch of the circumstances as they will always live in my memory.

Before going to Washington (which I did chiefly for the sake of hearing Mr Webster) I was told that in arguing the case at Exeter, N.H. he had left the whole court room "in tears" at the conclusion of his speech.

This, I confess, struck me unpleasantly – any attempt at pathos on a purely legal question like this seemed hardly in good taste. On my way to Washington I made the acquaintance of Mr Webster; we were together for some days in Philadelphia at the house of a common friend; and as the "College question" was one of ~~the~~ deep interest to literary men, we conversed often and largely on the subject. As he dwelt upon the leading points of the case in terms so calm, simple and precise, I said to myself, more than once, in reference to the story I had heard, "Whatever may have seemed appropriate in defending the College at _home_, and on her own ground, there will be no appeal to the feelings of Judge Marshall and his associates at Washington." The Supreme Court of the United States held its session that winter in a mean apartment of moderate size, the Capitol not having been rebuilt after its destruction 1814.º The audience, when the case came on, was therefore small, consisting chiefly of legal men, the "_élite_" of the profession throughout the country. Mr Webster entered upon his argument in the calm tone of easy and dignified conversation. His matter was so completely at his command that he scarcely looked at his brief, but went on for more than four hours with a statement so luminous and a chain of reasoning so easy to be understood and yet approaching so nearly to absolute demonstration, that he seemed to carry with him every man of his audience without the slightest effort or weariness on either side. It was hardly _eloquence_ in the strict sense of the term, it was pure reason. Now and then for a sentence ~~or two~~, his eye flashed and his voice swelled into a bolder note as he uttered some emphatic ~~thought~~, but he instantly fell back into the tone of earnest ~~conversation~~ which ran throughout the great body of ~~the~~ speech. A single ~~circumstance~~ will show you the clearness and absorbing power of his argument. [~~Judge Story, as I remarked at the opening of the case, prepared himself pen in hand, to take copious minutes. Hour after hour I saw him fixed in the same attitude,~~

A

~~but not a note on his paper~~ the argument closed and he had not taken a ~~single note. And the one who spoke to him afterwards of the fact with surprise remarked,~~ ~~Every thing was so clear, so easy to remember, that not a note seemed necessary. In fact I thought nothing about my notes."~~

The argument ended: Mr Webster stood ~~for some moments~~ silent before the court, while every eye was fixed intently upon him: At length ~~turned~~ addressing ~~to C. J. Marshall~~ ~~pronounced this~~ ~~judgment~~ he paid, "This, Sir, is my case! It is the case not merely of that humble institution, it is the case of every college in our Land! It is more! It is the case of every eleemosynary institution throughout our country – of all those great charities founded by the piety of our ancestors to alleviate human misery, and scatter blessings along the pathway of life! It is more! It is, in some sense, the case of every man among us who has property of which he may be stripped, for the question is simply this, "Shall our State Legislatures be allowed to take that which is not their own, to turn it from its original use, and apply it to such ends and purposes as they in their discretion shall see fit!"

Sir, you may destroy this little institution; it is weak, it is in your hands! I know it is one of the lesser lights in the literary horizon of our country. You may put it out! But if you do so, you must carry through your work! You must extinguish, one after another, all those great lights of science which for more than a century have thrown their radiance over our Land! It is, Sir, as I have said, a small college. And yet there are those who love it!" ~~Here the~~ feelings which he had thus far succeeded in keeping down, broke forth. His lips quivered; his firm cheeks trembled with emotion; his eyes were filled with tears; his voice choked; and he seemed struggling to the utmost, simply to gain that mastery over himself which might save him from an unmanly burst of feeling. I will not attempt to give the few broken words of tenderness in which he went on to speak of his attachment to the college. It seemed to be mingled throughout with all the recollections of father, mother, brothers, and all the trials and preventions through which he had made his way into life. Every one saw that it was wholly unpremeditated — a pressure on his heart which sought relief in words and tears. Recovering himself, after "a few moments, and turning to Judge Marshall, he said, Sir, I know not "how others may feel, (glancing at the opponents of the college before him) "for myself, when I see my *Alma Mater* surrounded, like Cesar in the "senate house, by those who are reiterating stab upon stab, I would "not for this right hand have her say to me," *Et tu quoque, mi fili!*

He sat down, and I need not tell you that the whole court room at Washington, as at Exeter, was in tears. It has always struck me, in looking back to that scene, that the pathetic depends not so much on the words themselves, as upon the estimate we put of him who utters them. No one was ashamed to weep when he saw before him the man who had made such an argument, melted into the tenderness of a child.

I am with much respect,

Very truly yours,

Chauncy A. Goodrich.

Hon: Rufus Choate,
Boston, Massachusetts.

G. 41. 19

added by Goodrich or by the amanuensis at Goodrich's specification. It is of particular interest that neither Goodrich nor Choate, in his later editing, in any way touched the Webster quotations.

But then we come to the interpolation of various words, and here we are on firm ground, because it is not only indicated that they were done with Goodrich's own pen but were positively done in his handwriting. The first one is in the third line of the third page. Over a caret Goodrich wrote, "he remarked." In the sixth line from the bottom on the same page, he inserted the word "he" over a caret. In the first line of page 4, again over a caret, he wrote "What he said" which later was crossed out by Choate who wrote in the words "The whole." In the fifth line of that same page he wrote in the word "sought." And, finally, at the beginning of the next to last line, he wrote in the words "before him." The significant part of this editing lies in two factors: that Goodrich, after the first two paragraphs about his own book, very carefully re-read his letter, and that the hand that signed the letter was the same hand that did the editing.

The professor had been doubly careful. He wrote the letter and then painstakingly edited it. Certainly he would neither have written the letter nor used quotes unless he was sure of his ground. In the second place, we can be reassured of his convictions regarding Webster's words by the fact that in editing the letter he made many changes but he did not touch the Webster quotations.

Right at this point I was completely satisfied that Webster had indeed used the small college phrase just as reported by Goodrich. But would others be convinced?

Continuing research brought a surprising jolt. It came from the discovery that twenty-five years previously the words of the original letter had appeared in a small circulation trade publication known as *The Quarterly Journal of Speech*. The article was written by John W. Black of Kenyon College. Word for word it duplicated the restored copy that had been so laboriously brought to its original state.

Dr. Black, in 1963, was Professor of Speech and Hearing at Ohio State University. Once a teacher of rhetoric, he had turned to the highly technical subject of voice and hearing. He became a recognized authority on phonetics. When he wrote his article for *The Quarterly Journal of Speech*, he was an instructor in rhetoric at Kenyon College. As a specialist in elocution he had a particular interest in Rufus Choate. His thesis for his master's degree had been on Choate.

How did he get a copy of the original Goodrich letter as it existed before Choate did his editing and rearranging? He obtained a copy by the simple process of going to the Boston Public Library. There an associate and he, one reading and the other writing, were able to look under the various pasteovers made by Choate and copy the letter as originally written by Goodrich.

Along with the jolt came a lift. It was a thrilling new clue that might easily remove all doubts. No matter how much logical theory there was in the research and no matter how much circumstantial evidence, there was still that thirty-four year spread between the time of the dramatic scene at Washington and the time that Goodrich wrote the letter to Choate. It was the opinion of Professor Black that the Goodrich letter containing the Webster quotes was not a first recording of the quotations by Goodrich, but was a copy of a record that he had written at a previous time.

Black quoted from a book by E. G. Parker titled *Reminiscences of Rufus Choate,* published in 1860. The reminiscences were written in diary fashion—a date and then a reporting of some incident or conversation. Parker, who was a junior partner in Choate's law firm, wrote in his book, "I studied him every day of my life for ten years." He also said, "To deepen the impressions of his thoughts and suggestions, *they were always committed to paper on returning home.*"

Under the date of December 20, 1852, three months after Webster's death, Mr. Parker quoted Rufus Choate as saying, "He [Wirt] told me [Choate] once that he sat right behind Webster in the Dartmouth College Case, and he didn't hear anything of that pathetic peroration which Goodrich describes; at least he wasn't impressed with anything in particular about it."

Wirt died in 1834. Therefore, his remark could not have been based on the Goodrich letter of 1852. It must have been based on a prior description. The only way to understand that Wirt was not impressed by the peroration is to remember that he not only was Webster's opponent but perhaps was much preoccupied in making notes for his defense argument. Wirt himself wrote, April 28, 1819, to Webster, "My argument was framed under great disadvantage, having to prepare it very hastily and under the pressure of a load of official business which was wholly new to me."[2] Also, he probably was not interested in Webster's deviation from the legal points involved.

Black observed, "The most important implication is that Goodrich apparently made some report of the peroration prior to the death of Wirt in 1834. This would indicate that Goodrich's letter to Choate was not the unpremeditated reminiscence of a man of sixty-two of an event which occurred when he was twenty-seven, but was an edition of an earlier, undiscovered report." This would mean that the undiscovered report might have been written an hour or so after the trial, or at the very latest, sometime during the sixteen years that Wirt survived after the case. In other words, there was no longer a thirty-four year span but one of not more than sixteen years or perhaps no span at all.

When had Goodrich described the peroration prior to his letter to Choate? To whom had his record been addressed?

Although Goodrich said in his letter that he had gone to Washington chiefly for the sake of hearing Webster, it could have been that he also was interested in making a report to Yale College, which certainly had a vital interest in the case. Perhaps Goodrich had written to Jeremiah Day, who at that time was president of Yale. A search for such evidence revealed ten letters from Goodrich to President Day, but none of them had anything to do with the Dartmouth College case. Perhaps the future will reveal more facts. As it is now, we know only that Goodrich had at least once described the peroration long before he wrote the letter to Choate.

The indication that Goodrich had written the Webster quotes before, suddenly brought to memory the block quotes used in Goodrich's letter. What are block quotes? They are quotation marks put in the lefthand margin, line after line. They are not just a whim. They are one of the many eccentricities peculiar to some practices of the printing art. They were used, for years, by some printers to denote an exact copy or a long quotation. This was done instead of using two quotation marks, one at the beginning and one at the end of the quoted material. The block quotes in the Goodrich letter along the lefthand margin were particularly noticeable because they were so unnecessary.

2. *Daniel,* 1930.

In the body of the text all the necessary quotes had been used. Was Goodrich saying that the quotations were copied from something previously written? If so, that would be very exciting. Had Goodrich used block quotes before? Was there anything to indicate that when he used them, he was not putting them down for the first time but was copying the quotes?

Even the most meager search reveals many examples of block quotes. To take one associated with this narrative, in Timothy Farrar's report of Dartmouth College vs. Woodward, there are many examples both of block quotes and of quotes within the text. The block quotes seemed to be an identification of passages that were quoted from printed documents such as the Constitution of the United States and the laws of New Hampshire, and the recorded statements of individuals.

A standard work on typography, *The Practice of Typography* by Theodore Low De Vinne, refers to block quotes in the volume titled *Correct Composition*. In the second edition, 1902, Mr. De Vinne says,

There have been authors who held that quotemarks at the beginning and the end of an extract extending over one or more pages were not emphatic enough to catch the eye of a casual reader. To prevent any misunderstanding as to the limit of the quotation, doubled commas were inserted at the beginning of every line by many printers of the first half of the nineteenth century. Nor is this fashion entirely obsolete; doubled commas at the beginning of lines are used occasionally in legal documents and in the columns of newspapers, but this style is out of fashion in good book-work. The long quotation or extract is specially indented or is shown in a smaller type, with equal clearness to the reader and with better effect in the print, but when double quotes are clearly marked in copy, the compositor must insert them without question.

When an author objects to quote-marks at the beginning of every line of a long extract or document, but insists on its appearance in the type of the text, the distinction desired for this extract may be made by indenting all the lines one em on each side or by a deeper indention on the left.

As an example De Vinne gives this reprinting of a letter written by America's most distinguished printer, Benjamin Franklin, but set to type by someone else.

The purchase of the Octavo Abridgment of Dr. Webster's American Dictionary, was one of the most important events of my life. My children have therefore requested me to draw up a written account of the circumstances attending it. This I shall do in the present paper. I begin with copying a statement which I prepared early in the year 1835, in the following words.

Statement.

" In the month of July 1828, about four months before
" the Quarto American Dictionary, was published, Mr. Converse
" made a proposal to commence an Abridgment in the Octavo
" form, that the latter might appear soon after the former. He
" urged with great earnestness to have this work committed to
" Joseph E. Worcester Esq, and offered to bear a large part of
" the expense. Dr. Webster felt so much perplexed and agitated
" by this subject, in his feeble state of health, that he called
" on me and stated, that unless something could be done
" to take this burden from his mind, and to relieve him from
" all further connection with Mr. Converse, he feared he should
" not live even to complete the printing of the Quarto Dictionary.
" He then dropped the suggestion, that he wished some one of
" his children was able and willing to pay him the fair value
" of the copyright of the proposed Octavo Abridgment, and
" take the whole concern from his hands.
" I had, at that time no property except my house; but consid
" ering this as a pointed intimation of his wishes that I would
" relieve him from this burden, I felt bound after conversing

"Philadᵃ July 5, 1775.

"Mr. Strahan,

"You are a Member of Parliament, and one
"of that Majority which has doomed my Country to de-
"struction,—You have begun to burn our Towns and
"murder our People,—Look upon your Hands!—They
"are stained with the Blood of your Relations!—You and
"I were long Friends:—You are now my Enemy,—and
"I am,
"Yours,
"B. Franklin."

Carl Van Doren in his *Life of Benjamin Franklin*, 1938, says that the fore-going letter was never sent. William Strahan, to whom the letter was written, had been a close friend of Dr. Franklin. The letter was not addressed to "Dear Sir," or "Dear Friend," or "Dear Straney" as was customary. Franklin was writing from America after his return from England and was expressing his indignation because Strahan in Parliament had seen the Americans as rebels and had voted against them with the Ministry.

The remote possibility that there was a record that Goodrich may have used block quotes before led straight and hurriedly back to the Historical Manuscripts Division of the Yale University Library and the Goodrich papers. There a document jumped out. At the request of his children, Goodrich was recording the terms of his agreement in regard to the purchase of the Octavo Abridgement of Dr. Webster's *American Dictionary*. He said, "I begin with copying a statement which I prepared early in the year 1835, in the following words." Then followed the statement with the block quotes down the lefthand margin. Goodrich did not need to put line after line of block quotes for he had said, "I begin with copying . . ." Here was magic confirmation that Goodrich, a careful man of habit, had not idly used the block quotes in the letter to Choate. He was deliberately saying, "I am copying."

The exhibit of the block quote shown here was written by an amanuensis and not by Goodrich himself. The block quotes were either dabbed in by Goodrich himself or on instruction from him. The facsimile is the first of a half dozen pages of the agreement. It is shown here to illustrate block quotes. The wording of the page is irrelevant.

In the first place, the letter, from such a source as Goodrich, would not have been written at all without ample reason. In the second place, Goodrich edited it very carefully and made no change in the quotations. In the third place, Choate himself completely accepted the words of Webster as reported by Goodrich. And last, but not least, the use of the block quotes established the fact that Goodrich had written the quotations before and was merely copying from sentences written previously. The conclusion is that we can accept Webster's phrase exactly as reported by Goodrich: "It is, Sir, as I have said, a small college. And yet *there are those who love it!*"

EPILOGUE

Daniel Webster—The Legend

AT seven o'clock on Sunday morning, October 24, 1852, the people of Marshfield heard the great bell of the parish church ringing violently —the traditional signal that a death had occurred in the community. Then followed three times three strokes, indicating that a male person had died. After that, the bell tolled slowly seventy times, to denote the age of the deceased. There was not a man or woman within its sound who did not know what it meant. Their great neighbor and leader would be among them no more."[1]

On the following Friday, October 29, all business ceased in Boston about forty miles to the north. The schools closed; there were no classes at Harvard; buildings were draped in black. Although Webster had asked for a quiet unostentatious funeral, thousands of people set out early for Marshfield—many of them by railroad and others by steamboat. It was estimated that from the nearby countryside as many as 2,000 carriages conveyed people to pay the last tribute.

"The completest man" wrote Ralph Waldo Emerson in his Journal. "Nature has not in our days . . . cut out such a masterpiece."

The legend of Daniel Webster is to an important degree built around his lifelong record as "The Defender of the Constitution." In that role he was doomed to make enemies as well as friends. A striking example of this was his Seventh of March speech (1850). He admitted that the Constitution had taken slavery for granted and had made allowances for its continued existence. However, he maintained that Congress could "prohibit the further introduc-

1. *Daniel*, 1930.

49

tion of slavery into its own territories."[2] Thus while tolerating slavery in the original states, he violently opposed its spread to future states. This stand made enemies among the abolitionists of the North while also making enemies in the South. A decade after Webster had gone, Lincoln was standing firmly on Webster's precept that the Union came first.

In the days of Webster, it was common practice to vilify political opponents both in the press and from the speaker's platform. The great Daniel was no exception. He was wide open to such attacks. He was neither "saint nor sinner." Especially in financial matters he was subjected to criticism. In the first place, he was always land-poor. He not only maintained the old family homestead in New Hampshire and the continually growing home at Marshfield in the Cape Cod area, but he bought unneeded land in the Midwest. He could not support these projects on what was then a Senator's pitifully small income. As a result he accepted financial aid from individuals whose backing raised questions as to what we would now call conflict of interest. Claude M. Fuess, the eminent Webster biographer, wrote ". . . there is no evidence whatever to show that he ever took bribes or diverted public funds to his own use, or, indeed, that his attitude toward legislation was ever affected by sinister motives."

Almost half a century (in 1900) after Webster had departed, ninety-seven scholars were asked to vote for men to be honored in the national Hall of Fame at New York University. All ninety-seven voted for Washington, ninety-six voted for Lincoln and for Webster, ninety-four voted for Franklin, and ninety-one chose Jefferson. Perhaps that small cross section is an indication as to what history will say.

When Daniel Webster, in the Supreme Court, said the memorable phrase, he had proven the right of one small college to choose its own destiny. Freedom to choose was a lifetime privilege which Webster exercised, with conscience, in his own personal career. His propensity for being in the minority was possibly the very factor that will make history record him as great. His life was certainly proof positive that, in government, a strong political minority can temper the vagaries of popular opinion.

2. *Writings*, 1903.

Poet Robert Frost, a one-time Dartmouth undergraduate and long a lecturer there, in writing of his own choice of poetry as a career, said in "The Road Not Taken":

> Two roads diverged in a wood, and I—
> I took the one less traveled by,
> And that has made all the difference.

That philosophy might well have been said of Webster's choice to defend the Constitution instead of reaching for political power.

In Daniel Webster's days of private law practice he frequently found himself defending the indigent or the culpable. He elected to represent the original small college instead of John Wheelock's newly created university. Thus not only was he taking the more difficult side but was laying himself open to accusations of being a turncoat. He remained a firm Federalist when the party had almost completely lost its appeal. He became a Whig and stayed one until he died, even though he became a minority pleader in a minority party. He favored compromise in the interests of unity when the word "compromise" was repugnant to the voters. He spoke as an American when a failure to speak sectionally was political suicide. He became "The Defender of the Constitution" at a time when many were attacking one or more of its various provisions. He was for the Union above all else, when some northern states as well as some southern states were talking secession.

Poet Stephen Vincent Benét saw Webster as the defender of the underdog. In his wonderful poetic prose story of *The Devil and Daniel Webster*, he pictured Webster defending an erring Jabez Stone who had mortgaged his soul to the devil for a loan of money. Webster's opponent in court was the devil himself, who was claiming the sinner's soul when payment of the loan became due. Just to keep Webster in his familiar disadvantageous position, the jury was made up of the country's most notorious criminals, murderers, and skinflints. As Benét adds, after Webster had beaten the devil in court: "Every time there is a thunderstorm you can hear Webster's rolling voice in the hollows of the New Hampshire sky."

APPENDIX

The Goodrich Letter as Edited and Rearranged by Choate

THIS APPENDIX is included solely for the record. After the restoration of the Goodrich letter had been accomplished, the detail of Choate's alterations was no longer essential to the narrative. Then why include it? It is because the restoration of the original letter involved pulling apart an old, respected manuscript. It therefore seemed proper to present a report of the condition in which that letter was left by Rufus Choate. That manuscript earned its status by being the original of Choate's rearranged version of the Goodrich letter. As such it has been the standard reference work since 1853.

The facsimiles as produced by Carroll A. Wilson take the form of six pages. The first three are from the Goodrich letter as written by the Goodrich amanuensis. The remaining three illustrate both the additional paragraph written by Choate himself and the rewrites by Choate's amanuensis to accomplish changes of sequence.

Let us examine the pages from the Goodrich letter. They are easily identifiable both because they are in the handwriting of Goodrich's amanuensis and because the end of each page fits in with the beginning of the following page. Choate omitted the first page of Goodrich's letter because all except the last three lines were not germane to the description of the Supreme Court scene. However, the last three lines from page 1 of the restored letter (see Chapter v for the restored letter) were copied in Choate's own inimitable handwriting on the top of page 2 of the Goodrich letter. Thus it was that page 2 of the Goodrich letter became page 1 of the Choate rearrangement. These three lines read, "Before going to Washington (which I did chiefly for the sake of hearing Mr. Webster) I was told that in arguing the case at Exeter, N. H. he had 'left the whole courtroom in tears' at the conclusion of his speech."

At the bottom of that page is clearly illustrated some of the damage done to Goodrich's letter by the person who bound the letter into the Choate manuscript. There is a distortion in the last three lines so that the sentences do not read evenly.

On each of the three pages, the marks of Choate's heavy pen are clearly visible. On page II the Wilson facsimile reproduction fails to show the block quotes. This is because the manuscript was bound into book form on the left hand edge, thus destroying visibility. However, the block quotes do appear in an inconspicuous manner on page III. They might have gone unnoticed had there been no restoration of the original letter, through removing the letter from the binding.

With the second group of three pages the confusion began. On page IV is a simple overlay in the handwriting of Choate's clerk referring to the fact that Justice Story had not taken a single note. It was substantially a rewrite of what Goodrich had written and was written as an overlay for the purpose of changing the sequence.

Page V shows an overlay entitled "Goodrich 3" written partly in Choate's own handwriting and partly in the handwriting of his amanuensis. This is the new paragraph which Choate added. It reads as follows: "The court room during these 2 or 3 minutes presented an extraordinary spectacle. Chief Justice Marshall, with his tall and gaunt figure bent over as if to catch the slightest whisper, the deep furrows of his cheek expanded with emotion, and eyes suffused with tears; Mr. Justice Washington at his side, with his small and emaciated frame and countenance more like marble than I ever saw on any other human being—leaning forward with an eager, troubled look; and the remainder of the Court, at the two extremities, pressing as it were, toward a single point, while the audience below were wrapping themselves round in closer folds beneath the bench to catch each look, and every movement of the speaker's face. If a painter could give us the scene on canvas—those forms" Then it goes on in the writing of Choate's amanuensis beginning: "and countenances, and Daniel Webster as he stood there in the midst—it would be one of the most touching pictures in the history of eloquence."

Choate was reporting from friends who had been eye-witnesses of the court proceedings.

The balance of the page, in the handwriting of Choate's amanuensis, is merely a rewriting of Goodrich's closing paragraph which Choate placed in an earlier sequence.

Page VI is a continuation of the bottom paragraph of page V as written by Choate's amanuensis.

The three overlays were tipped in with paste and did not interfere with Wilson's photographic reproduction, nor did they damage the last three pages of the original letter. However, there were overlays, tipped in by sealing wax. The sealing wax not only prevented Wilson from reproducing the first page of Goodrich's letter but also made the restoration of that page difficult. If one will refer to the restoration in Chapter V, the marks of the wax will be discernible.

To add further to the possible confusion, there was one overlay presented in the manuscript which did not appear in Wilson's facsimiles. That one overlay, unlike the others, was written on both sides of a single sheet of paper.

The front side was largely made up of notes by Choate's amanuensis, written to himself, two of which were designated as "alteration." There were two items of inter-

Section 1st

[top lines illegible crossed-out draft]

This, I confess, struck me unpleasantly — any attempt at pathos on a purely legal question like this seemed hardly in good taste. On my way to Washington I made the acquaintance of Mr Webster; we were together for some days in Philadelphia at the house of a common friend; and as the "College question" was one of the deep interest to literary men, we conversed often and largely on the subject. As he dwelt upon the leading points of the case in terms so calm, simple and precise, I said to myself, more than once, in reference to the story I had heard, "whatever may have seemed appropriate in defending the College at home, and on her own ground, there will be no appeal to the feelings of Judge Marshall and his associates at Washington". The Supreme Court of the United States held its session that winter in a mean apartment of moderate size, the Capitol not having been rebuilt after its destruction in 1814. The audience, when the case came on, was therefore small, consisting chiefly of legal men, the élite of the profession throughout the country. Mr Webster entered upon his argument in the calm tone of easy and dignified conversation. His matter was so completely at his command that he scarcely looked at his brief, but went on for more than four hours with a statement so luminous and a chain of reasoning so easy to be understood and yet approaching so nearly to absolute demonstration, that he seemed to carry with him every man of his audience without the slightest effort or weariness on either side. It was hardly eloquence, not in the strict sense of the term, it was pure reason. Now and then for a sentence or two, his eye flashed and his voice swelled into a bolder note as he uttered some emphatic thought, but he instantly fell back into the tone of earnest conversation which ran throughout the great body

[lower lines fragmentary and crossed-out]

A

but not a note on his paper - the argument closed and he had not taken a single note. ~~Unlike~~ To one who spoke to him afterwards of the fact with surprise he remarked, "Every thing was so clear, so easy to remember, that not a note seemed necessary ~~& I never got~~ I thought nothing about my notes."

The argument ended: Mr Webster stood ~~motionless~~ for some moments silent before the court, while every eye was fixed intently upon him: At length ~~turning~~ addressing ~~Chief Justice Marshall~~ ~~he~~ ~~the C. J. Marshall~~ he said "This, Sir, is my case! It is the case not merely of that humble institution, it is the case of every college in our Land! It is more! It is the case of every eleemosynary institution throughout our country - of all those great charities founded by the piety of our ancestors to alleviate human misery, and scatter blessings along the pathway of life! It is more! It is, in some sense, the case of every man among us who has property of which he may be stripped, for the question is simply this, "Shall our State Legislatures be allowed to take that which is not their own, to turn it from its original ~~use~~ and apply it to such ends and purposes as they in their discretion shall see fit!"

"Sir, you may destroy this little institution; it is weak, it is in ~~your~~ hands! I know it is one of the lesser lights in the literary horizon of ~~our~~ country. You may put it out! But if you do so, you must carry through your work! You must extinguish, one after another, all those great lights of science which for more than a century have thrown their radiance over our Land!   It is, Sir, as I have said, a small college. And yet there are those who love it!" ~~Here~~ Here the feelings which he had thus far succeeded in keeping down, broke forth. His lips quivered; his firm cheeks trembled with emotion; his eyes were filled with tears; his voice choked; and he seemed struggling to the utmost, simply to gain that mastery over himself which might save him from an unmanly burst of feeling. I will not attempt to give the few broken words of tenderness in which

II

he went on to speak of his attachment to the college. It seemed to be mingled throughout with all the recollections of father, mother, brothers, and all the trials and preventions through which he had made his way into life. Every one saw that it was wholly unpremeditated — a pressure on his heart which sought relief in words and tears. Recovering himself, after "a few moments, and turning to Judge Marshall, he said "Sir, I know not "how others may feel, (glancing at the opponents of the college ~~he said~~) "for myself when I see my Alma Mater surrounded, like Cesar in the "senate house, by those who are reiterating stab upon stab, I would "not for this right hand have her say to me, "Et tu quoque, mi fili.""

He sat down, and I need not tell you that the whole court room at Washington, as at Exeter, was in tears. It has always struck me, in looking back to that scene, that the pathetic depends not so much on the words themselves, as upon the estimate we put on him who utters them. No one was ashamed to weep when he saw before him the men who had made such an argument, melted into the tenderness of a child.

I am with much respect,
Very truly yours,
Chauncy A. Goodrich.

Hon. Rufus Choate,
Boston, Massachusetts.

1° Alteration. after the words, "the power of his argument," ~~substituted as follows~~

A.

I observed that Judge Story, at the opening of the case had prepared himself pen in hand, as if to take copious minutes. Hour after hour, I saw him fixed in the same attitude, but so far as I could perceive with not a note on his paper — the argument closed and I could not discover ~~that~~ he had taken a single note. Others around me remarked the same thing; & it was a ~~many~~ the ~~report~~ of Washington, that a friend spoke to him of the fact with surprise, when the Judge remarked, "Every thing was so clear, so easy to remember, that not a note seemed necessary; in fact, I thought little or nothing about my notes!" A.

speech, _____ _____ _____ _____ _____, giving in its place an extract from Cicero, which he probably regarded as a more appropriate conclusion of a strictly legal argument. No hand but his could ever reproduce it; ~~and~~ I am sure you will be interested in a slight sketch of the ca_____ _____ a___ e___ill always live in my memory. _____ chiefly for the sake of hearing Before going ___ ___ Story, which Phipare at Exeter, N.H. he had (Mr Webster) I was told that in arguing the conclusion of his speech. "left the whole court room in tears" at

A.

The Court room during these [2 or 3] minutes
presented an extraordinary spectacle. Chief Justice
Marshall, with his tall gaunt figure
bent over as if to catch the slightest whisper,
the deep [furrows] of his cheek expanded with emotion,
& his eyes suffused with tears. [Mr.] Justice
Washington at his side, with his small
& emaciated figure, & countenance more
like marble than [life]... [every] human being leaning forward with
an eager [attentive] look... the remainder were
[...] at the extremities, passing
as [a fixed] [blank]; a single [word], [while]
the audience [were] busy [in] [fixing] themselves
[...] [against] the [...]
[...] each [...] [every] [movement] of the
speaker's face — No [painter] [could] [give] [us]
[...] the [scene] — [those] [forms],

+ countenances & Daniel Webster as he
stood in the midst, it would be one of
most touching pictures in the history of
eloquence. One thing it taught me, that
the pathetic depends not merely on the words
uttered, but still more on the estimate we
put upon him who utters them. There was
not one among the strong-minded men of that
assembly who could ~~feel~~ think it ~~make~~ unmanly
to weep, when he saw standing before him
the man who had made such an argum[ent]
melted into the tenderness of a child. Mr.
Webster had now recovered his composure; and fix[ed]
his keen eye on the C. Justice said in that deep tone
with which he sometimes thrilled the
heart of an audience; "Sir, I know no[...]
[...]

how others may feel" (glancing at the
opponents of the College before him) "but for
myself when I see my Alma Mater surrounded, like Cesar in the Senate House, by
those who are aiming stab upon stab,
I would not for this right hand have had
her turn to me & say, '*Et tu quoque, mi
fili!*'"

He sat down. There was a death-like
stillness throughout the room for some moments; every one seemed to be slowly recovering himself, & coming gradually back
back to his ordinary range of thought and
feeling. N.B. ~~~~~~~~~~~~

[crossed-out paragraph, largely illegible]
I cannot hit the ... ...

[left margin fragments]
he went
mingled
and ...
into life
on his ...
"... ...
"how oth
"for mys
"senate"
"not for ...
room a
me, ...
so much
him wh
before him
the mee
tender

Hon
B ...

[bottom of page]
... after ...
pressure upon his heart which sought relief
in words & tears" — substitute the following
~~the ... ...~~ to the close. B The
Court-room during these 2 or 3 minutes
presented an extraordinary spectacle. Judge

est in that overlay. One was a line set off by parentheses: "I give the substance and in many instances the exact words. The whole occupied not more than 6 or 8 minutes." By "the whole" he, of course, meant the peroration. Some on-the-spot observers had said that the peroration was short. But what is short after an argument of more than four hours? Choate was exact. He had discussed the case with enough people to be on firm ground. The other item was of minor interest. The amanuensis wrote: "Sir, this is my case." When the line was finally written, it appeared in just the way that Goodrich had reported: "This, Sir, is my case."

The reverse side of the overlay showed Choate writing "The C. J." (Chief Justice) and then crossing out the whole paragraph. He copied it in his own handwriting. This appears on page v, titled "Goodrich 3". It begins: "The court room during these 2 or 3 minutes presented an extraordinary spectacle. Chief Justice Marshall . . ." This was the paragraph that Choate added.

Both the front and reverse sides showed the marks of sealing wax. Their counterparts do not show on the pages shown in this appendix. They do show on page 1 of the restored Goodrich letter as it appears in the last chapter. This was the page that Choate omitted. It was used to carry overlays. These two overlays are not shown here because they were superseded by rewrites as already shown.

As has been said, Choate did not change the meaning of the letter in any way. Almost all of the underlines were carefully followed. They took the form of italics in the Choate pamphlet. Goodrich had double underlined the expression "Alma Mater," but Choate did not italicize those words. On the other hand, Goodrich in the last paragraph of his letter did not underline the word "pathetic," but Choate in the printed pamphlet italicized the word. However, there are at least two changes that are worth a special comment.

On page iv in this appendix—about half-way down the page—Choate crossed out the words "on dits" and in his own pen wrote the word "reports." The phrase thus read, "among the reports of Washington . . ." When this line appeared in the *New-York Daily Times* of July 30, 1853, and also in Choate's pamphlet, the words "on dits" had been reinstated. This could easily lead one to the conclusion that the whole letter, so mixed with overlays, had been redrafted for the address at Hanover and ultimately for the printer of the pamphlet. Fortunately, however, the original Goodrich letter, and not any new draft, was bound into the complete manuscript of Choate's speech.

Choate did make one change that was decidedly for the worse. On the last page of the original letter (page iii in this appendix) Goodrich quoted Webster as saying, "I would not for this right hand have her say to me 'Et tu quoque, mi fili!' " Choate, in the final manuscript, had added a translation of the Latin phrase, so that it read: "Et tu quoque, mi fili! And thou too, my son!" This unfortunate translation does not appear in the facsimile in this appendix. It did, however, appear both in the *New-York*

Daily Times report and in Choate's pamphlet. This was further evidence that there had been a redraft before the speech at Hanover and before the manuscript was given over to the printer of the pamphlet.

Choate, in effect, made Webster guilty of a banality. Why did Choate add that translation? Could he have been thinking of the undergraduates that would be listening to his memorial address? Let's hope not. Perhaps he was thinking of the townspeople and the farmers who would appear in Hanover from far and wide.

It was common practice for Webster to use Latin phrases in his speeches but never once, to my knowledge, did he give an English translation. Of one thing we may be sure: Webster would not have translated such a simple phrase for the learned Supreme Court of the United States. That is one point, at least, on which this study can rest indefinitely.

List of Works Consulted

Arranged in chronological order

Report of the Case of the Trustees of Dartmouth College against William H. Woodward, Timothy Farrar, Portsmouth, N. H.: John W. Foster; Boston: West, Richardson, and Lord, 1819.

Speeches and Forensic Arguments, Daniel Webster, 2 vols., Boston: Perkins, Marvin, and Co., vol. 1, 1830; vol. 2, 1835.

The Works of Daniel Webster, 6 vols., Boston: Little, Brown & Co., 1851.

A Discourse delivered before the Faculty, Students and Alumni of Dartmouth College on the Day preceding Commencement, July 27, 1853, commemorative of Daniel Webster, Rufus Choate, Boston and Cambridge: J. Munroe and Co., 1853.

(Eulogy on Daniel Webster in) *A Memorial of Daniel Webster from the City of Boston*, ed. G. S. Hillard, Boston: Little, Brown & Co., 1853.

The Private Correspondence of Daniel Webster, ed. Fletcher Webster, 2 vols., Boston: Little, Brown & Co., 1857.

Reminiscences of Rufus Choate, The Great American Advocate, Edwin Griffin Parker, New York: Mason Brothers, 1860.

A Discourse Commemorative of Chauncey A. Goodrich, D.D., Theodore Dwight Woolsey, 1860.

Select British Eloquence, Chauncey A. Goodrich, New York: Harper & Bros., 1861.

Life of Daniel Webster, George Ticknor Curtis, 2 vols., New York: D. Appleton and Co., 1870.

The First Half Century of Dartmouth College: being historical collections and personal reminiscences, Nathan Crosby, Hanover, N. H.: J. B. Parker, 1876.

The History of Dartmouth College, Baxter Perry Smith, Boston: Houghton, Osgood and Co., 1878.

(Address by Stephen Allen in) *The Webster Centennial. Proceedings of the Webster Historical Society at Marshfield, Massachusetts, October 12, 1882*, ed. Thomas Harrison Cummings, Boston: Webster Historical Society, 1883.

Daniel Webster, Henry Cabot Lodge, Boston and New York: Houghton Mifflin & Co., 1883.

A History of Dartmouth College and the town of Hanover, N. H., F. Chase, ed. J. K. Lord, 2 vols., Cambridge, Mass.: J. Wilson & Sons, 1891–1913. Vol. 2 has title & imprint: *A History of Dartmouth College, 1815–1909*, J. K. Lord, being the second volume of *A History . . . New Hampshire*, begun by Frederick Chase, Concord, N. H.: The Rumford Press, 1913.

Dartmouth Traditions, William Carrol Hill, Hanover: Dartmouth Press, 1901.

The Proceedings of the Webster Centennial, ed. Ernest Martin Hopkins, Hanover, N. H.: Dartmouth Press, 1902.

Daniel Webster, John Bach McMaster, New York: The Century Co., 1902.

The Letters of Daniel Webster, ed. Claude Halstead Van Tyne, New York: McClure, Phillips, & Co., 1902.

The Writings and Speeches of Daniel Webster, The National Edition, 18 vols., Boston: Little Brown, & Co., 1903.

Daniel Webster, The Expounder of the Constitution, Everett Pepperrell Wheeler, New York and London: G. P. Putnam, 1905.

General Catalogue of Dartmouth College and The Associated Schools 1769–1910, *including a historical sketch of the college*, ed. Charles Franklin Emerson, Hanover, N. H., printed for the college 1910–1911.

Reminiscences of the Elegy of Rufus Choate on Webster delivered at Dartmouth College, July 26, 1853, and discursions more or less therewith connected, Charles Caverno, Boston: Sherman, French, & Co., 1914.

The Story of Dartmouth, Wilder D. Quint, Boston: Little, Brown & Co., 1914.

John Marshall and The Constitution, A Chronicle of the Supreme Court, E. S. Corwin, New Haven: Yale University Press, 1919.

Rufus Choate, the Wizard of the Law, Claude Moore Fuess, New York, Minton Balch & Co., 1928.

Daniel Webster, Allan L. Benson, New York: Cosmopolitan Book Corporation, 1929.

Daniel Webster, Claude Moore Fuess, 2 vols., Boston: Little, Brown & Co., 1930.

History of Dartmouth College, Leon Burr Richardson, 2 vols., Hanover, N. H.: Dartmouth College Publications, 1932.

"Webster's Peroration in the Dartmouth College Case", John W. Black, *The Quarterly Journal of Speech*, vol. XXIII, no. 4, Dec. 1937.

"Daniel Webster and Dartmouth", Carroll A. Wilson, *The Colophon*, new series, vol. III, no. 1, winter 1938.

"Daniel Webster and Dartmouth," Carroll A. Wilson, *Dartmouth Alumni Magazine*, April 1943.

This Our Purpose, Ernest Martin Hopkins, Hanover, N. H.: Dartmouth Publications, 1950.

Raymond of the Times, Ernest Francis Brown, New York: Norton, 1951.

The Development and Scope of Higher Education in the United States, Richard Hofstadter and C. DeWitt Hardy, New York: Columbia University Press, for the Commission on Financing Higher Education, 1952.

Bartlett's Familiar Quotations, 13th and centennial edition, Boston: Little Brown & Co., 1955.

Profiles in Courage, John F. Kennedy, New York: Harper, 1956.

Hanover, New Hampshire, a bicentennial book, ed. Francis Lane Childs, Hanover, N. H.: Hanover Bicentennial Committee, 1961.

The American College and University, a History, by Frederick Rudolph, New York: Knopf, 1962.

Index

One thousand copies of this book
have been printed at The Stinehour Press.
Illustrations have been reproduced by
The Meriden Gravure Company.
This is copy number

371